The Barthes Effect

Theory and History of Literature
Edited by Wlad Godzich and Jochen Schulte-Sasse

For other books in the series, see p. 123

The Barthes Effect

The Essay as Reflective Text

Réda Bensmaïa

Translation by Pat Fedkiew

Foreword by Michèle Richman

Theory and History of Literature, Volume 54

University of Minnesota Press, Minneapolis

This book is published with the financial assistance of the Graduate School and the College of Liberal Arts of the University of Minnesota.

Published by the University of Minnesota Press
2037 University Avenue Southeast, Minneapolis MN 55414.
Published simultaneously in Canada
by Fitzhenry & Whiteside Limited, Markham.
Printed in the United States of America.

Library of Congress Cataloging-in-Publication Data

Bensmaïa, Réda.
   The Barthes effect

   (Theory and history of literature; v. 54)
   Translation of: Barthes à l'essai.
   Includes index.
   1. French essays—History and criticism.
2. Montaigne, Michel de, 1533–1592. Essais.
3. Montaigne, Michel de, 1533–1592—Influence.
4. Barthes, Roland. 5. Essay. I. Title. II. Series.
PQ731.B413 1987   844'.009   86-24938
ISBN 0-8166-1378-8
ISBN 0-8166-1379-6 (pbk.)

To Saliha

Contents

Foreword
Michèle Richman

In his inaugural address to the *Collège de France*, as first holder of the Chair of Literary Semiology, Roland Barthes described himself as a "fellow of doubtful nature, whose every attribute is somehow challenged by its opposite."[1] Thus his qualifications for that honorific position are presented with characteristic ambivalence:

> Though it is true that I long wished to inscribe my work within the field of science — literary, lexicological, and sociological — I must admit that I have produced *only* essays, an ambiguous genre in which analysis vies with writing. (*L*, 457, emphasis added)

Yet Barthes's diverse and extensive corpus of essays has probably contributed more vigorously to the renewal of that "anti-genre," as Réda Bensmaïa convincingly demonstrates, than that of any other contemporary writer. So how are we to interpret the self-deprecating "only"? According to context, as deference to science, or as an oblique hint at unfulfilled literary ambitions (a suspicion fueled by rumor that at the time of his death Barthes was engaged in writing a novel)? Should we simply dismiss it as circumstantial modesty? Indeed, what kind of confrontation is really being staged when Barthes sets analysis against writing, given that his own *écriture* exhibits complexities that the English term barely suggests? Moreover, we recall that Barthes repeatedly underscored the writer's "responsibility of form," so one must assume that his choice of a so-called ambiguous genre reflects a historically based decision as much as personal predilection.

The auto-critical introduction just cited appeared in 1977, only three years prior to the death of Barthes, and it reminds us that the posthumous evaluation of his work has just begun. With uncanny prescience he willed an inventory of his work to which critics must inevitably refer. The "lesson" (its original French title) comes to us in the form of an exemplary *essai*, weaving intellectual autobiography, anecdotal *punctum*, and discursive transgressions in a way that brilliantly manipulates the essay form to idiosyncratic ends. Thus, despite an increasing familiarity with Barthes thanks to a steady flow of translations, this address reminds us how he continues to defy the conventions of our critical idiom. Seasoned readers attuned to Barthes's playful neologisms, esoterisms, and untranslatables on the order of *"le frisson du sens"* (*RB*, 97) or *"une jouissance de l'idéologie"* (a pleasure of ideology, *RB*, 104), will be less disconcerted by declarations to the effect that "science can be born of fantasy" (*L*, 477) or "writing makes knowledge festive" (*L*, 464). But which department could accommodate a "phantasmic teaching" (*L*, 477) or, for that matter, a semiology defined as

> that labor which collects the impurity of language, the waste of linguistics, the immediate corruption of the message: nothing less than the desires, the fears, the appearances, the intimidations, the advances, the blandishments, the protests, the excuses, the aggressions, the various kinds of music out of which active language is made. (*L*, 470–471)

Finally, what will critics find to say about a writer so obsessed with words he claims to suffer an illness—"I *see* language" (*RB*, 161)?

The Barthes Effect, with its focus on the eccentric phenomenon of the essay within the history of poetic norms, enhances our appreciation of the polemical background signaled by Barthes's qualifying only. In his effort to track down the specificity of the genre's particular logic, Bensmaïa elucidates the negative definition of Barthes's ideal of the essay "without the dissertation" (*S/Z*, 5). Bensmaïa's immediate goal is to consider the essay as a practice of writing, rather than engage in an interpretive reading or commentary. Moreover, this treatment of an issue central to contemporary critical theory invites the reader to a general apprenticeship in the reading of modern texts. English-speaking readers in particular will be gratified by an elegant introduction to a mode of writing for which the French are perhaps better prepared—both to read and to respect.

Certainly Barthes's ambivalence is mild when compared with the reception offered the contemporary essay in English. According to one recent assessment,[2] the marketplace has demoted it to an even lower commercial value than poetry. If it has survived in England and America, it is through "duplicity." With Montaigne as common ancestor, the English essay exhibited for many generations the same characteristics as its French counterpart. Enjoying maximal fluidity, it was informal and familiar, with an "ameba-like" versatility often held together by little more than the author's voice. Primarily an urban genre, it allowed the author to use himself as starting point for digressions on the mundanity of everyday life, while dialoguing with an educated, homogeneous readership. Ironically, the most modern characteristic of Montaigne's essay – its patchwork of quotations – was also its only concession to tradition and authority.

Post-Montaigne, the essay split into two distinct modalities: one remained informal, personal, intimate, relaxed, conversational, and often humorous; the other, dogmatic, impersonal, systematic, and expository. This specialization is allegedly responsible for the diminished incisiveness and pungency of the essay at the turn of this century, leading to its modernist demotion to "belles-lettrism."

External factors must be recognized as well, including the eclipse of conversation as an art and its impact on a mode of writing that implies a speaking relationship between writer and reader; the collapse of the "fiction of the educated reader," whom old essayists seemed to be addressing; the prevalence of psychoanalysis as access to self-knowledge; and finally, the technical specialization undermining the essayist's ability to speak with the generalist's authority. By way of optimistic contrast, one can point to the renewal of the philosophical and speculative essay in Europe under the influence of Adorno, Benjamin, Simone Weil, Camus, Çioran, and Barthes. Nonetheless, this Nietzschean offspring, distinguished by a fragmentary, aphoristic critical writing, is only beginning to have an influence on American writing.

Bensmaïa offers a similar overview, albeit from the vantage point of the poetician, in which historical tendencies are refracted through formal trends. Thus the bifurcation after Montaigne into the critical versus biographical essay is examined only as it is mirrored within Barthes's own career. The revival of the genre indicated above is also expressed somewhat differently. In his own words, Bensmaïa wants the Barthesian essay to be appreciated as having "reconquered" a genre born with Montaigne, but which now attains a status entirely its own. With Barthes, the essay makes its entry into the history of literature as a "reflective text," one which goes to the extreme of destroying its own discursive category.

Yet the full realization of this goal is evidenced only in the later, post-*S/Z* writings. Bensmaïa argues that *S/Z* marks a break – though not of the fundamental ideological sort connoted by the term in the lexicons of Althusser and Foucault – between the earlier critical essay and the subsequent fragment-texts. The latter display common modifications along the analysis/writing axis. Instead of external stimuli, the writer establishes himself as primary intellectual object for eclectic digressions. Correlatively, the writer's *écriture* is foregrounded because of an added emphasis on questions of language in relation to a subject whose singularity has become increasingly problematic. The displacement of the structural analysis of narrative by the readerly/writerly distinction announced in *S/Z* appears to have also precipitated an internal shift. Whereas the move from "work" to "text" may document Barthes's disaffection with structuralist models and proposes alternative "poststructuralist" notions, Bensmaïa eschews these catch phrases in order to better appreciate how the critical essay is transformed along the more intimate vein of Montaigne, closer to self-portrait than ideological polemic. Somewhere between the two possibilities, Bensmaïa locates the specificity of the later Barthes.

The exclusive concentration on *The Pleasure of the Text, A Lover's Discourse, Roland Barthes by Roland Barthes, and Camera Lucida* is further justified through the critical commonplace that discredits the notion of "one" Barthes by citing his "vertiginous displacements"—from psychoanalysis to linguistics to semiology. The passage through Marxism in *Mythologies* to the "pleasure of the text" appears to reinforce an opposition between the early and later writings, between politics and aesthetics, between ideology and hedonism. If there exists an underlying unity to the writings of Barthes, Bensmaïa discovers it in the final texts, where the secret ambition of the entire career is fulfilled: to bring together in one writing movement, in a single *Text*, modes of discourse that had hitherto been kept separate—that of the *écrivain* and that of the *écrivant* and also that of the "producer" (the Author) of the text and its "user" (page xxvi). The result is a double text that deconstructs the hierarchy between tutor text and "parasitical" commentary. The reflective text functions as an essay to the extent it speculates on a certain number of classical literary problems—narrative, structure, writing, and so on. As a practice of writing, the text is generated from fragments outside established classifications which refuse a fixed center or totalizing scheme. Their composition consists of heterogeneous series "hinged" together by a "*mot-bas-tant*," a "sufficient word," the most common being *le corps*—the body. Barthes's realization that the body is inseparable from language ("entanglement of language and the body: which begins?" [*RB*, 91]), and his experience of the body as mediated by already-written citations—this slippage from "*corpus*" to "*corps*" explains why "R.B." became the ultimate object of analysis for Roland Barthes.

But the inward turn of Barthes's later texts marks not only a modulation in register. It also repeats and renews the essay's possibilities as they have been explored by Montaigne, the German Romantics, and, more recently, Blanchot. As a complement to these historical precedents mentioned by Bensmaïa, we will consider three other moments in the recent history of the essay to better situate the contribution of Barthes.

On several occasions Barthes expressed enthusiasm for the early essays of Georges Bataille. In particular, the 1929 piece entitled "Le Gros Orteil" (The Big Toe) served as a springboard for reflections[3] which exemplify the characteristics of Barthes's later writings. Central to his appreciation was the fact that Bataille managed to sustain his discussion without recourse to psychoanalysis: "This text, which concerns a part of the body, discreetly but obstinately avoids psychoanalysis." Faithful to Bataille's subversive intentions, Barthes offers his own thoughts in the form of fragments—the "sorties" or exits from the text. Such fragmentation counters the concentration of knowledge into a single authoritative discourse, just

P of the Text – Appearance of the book prevents ascriptions typical of book → theme development – / Chapt heads.

as the separate blocks of writing can better resist unwanted associations or connections. The struggle with the recuperative power of the signified is like a "tactic without strategy." And the bellicose imagery is befitting, given that the text is conceived as a utopian space on which to arbitrate the warfare of languages.

Bataille waged his own struggle against the psychoanalytic "gendarme" by causing knowledge to erupt precisely where least expected. And in a gesture of solidarity, Barthes graphically demonstrates the pluralization of codes by dispersing his ideas among fragments arranged according to the most arbitrary order of all – the alphabet. We recall that Bataille's piece had appeared in *Documents*, an eclectic review of "Doctrines, Archaeologie, Beaux-Arts et Ethnographie" that started publication in 1929. Along with Michel Leiris, Bataille was a frequent contributor to a section of each issue entitled *Dictionnaire*, consisting of a parodic compilation of Flaubertian *"idées non-reçues"* or, more aggressively, *irrecevables*. Barthes admired these devastating glances at the underside of bourgeois-industrial civilization, even though his own transgressions never carried him quite so close to the oneiric absurdities of the quotidian. Among the most striking "documents" were photographs. One headed the dictionary's first entry – *abattoir* – by showing rows of neatly aligned cloven hoofs outside the slaughterhouse. Another, Boiffard's glossy print of a naked hairy toe, accompanied Bataille's entry. Both effectively highlighted the irony of the review's titular claim to objectivity.

Historically, the review reflects dissatisfaction with the confines of the critical essay, as evidenced in a commentary on Giacometti by Leiris.[4] After some thoughts on the nature of fetishism in our culture, and the ennui induced by most art, Leiris touts the value of crises as "those rare moments when the external world suddenly collapses and a veritable communication between inner sentiment and outer objects is possible." Then, slipping into the first-person singular, he declares, "I like Giacometti's sculpture because it is like the petrification of one of those crises." Nonetheless, he will not offer an explanation or justification for this preference along objective lines or criteria, since "I prefer *DIVAGUER* [to digress]." In place of the expected perfunctory summation, including predictions for the young sculptor's future, Leiris unfurls a long, nonlinear succession of magnificent divagations inspired by "these figures engendered by his [Giacometti's] fingers." Nearly half a century later, Barthes will give a lesson and contend that the only way to learn and to teach is through digression.

In his brief historical overview, Bensmaïa alludes to an appeal made by Sartre in 1943 to rescue the essay from its modern "crisis." Interestingly, Sartre's contention that the genre must renew itself by severing ties with classical discourse if it is to accommodate an experience of modernity – "for if we try to express our thoughts of today in the language of the past, what metaphors, what circumlocutions, what imprecise imagery" – had introduced his virulent attack on Bataille's *l'Expérience intérieure.*[5] Composed of Nietzschean fragments whose tortured syntax and disregard for narrative continuity heighten the drama of this scriptural mise-en-scène of self, the *Expérience* is compared to a "hybrid genre" cultivated by the Surrealists. Crossing philosophy with confession, Sartre declares, they produced *l'essai-martyr*. In their disdain for the tranquillity of writing, he continues, they claim to endow their enterprise with "the perilous seriousness of a veritable act; *Les Pensées, Les Confessions, Ecce Homo, Les Pas perdus, L'Amour four, Le Traité du style, L'Age d'homme*; it is within this series of impassioned geometries that *L'Expérience intérieure* takes its place."

More disturbing than the calculated shock effects, however, is the "carnal promiscuity" between author and reader fostered by the *essai-martyr*. Having discredited *l'expérience* of Bataille as refractory to any transcendent project, Sartre nonetheless admires the excruciating denuding of the man. In the end, he calls for a revised psychoanalysis to appreciate its transgressive modernity. Similarly, after exhausting a linguistic analysis of Bataille's semi-autobiographical fiction, *Histoire de l'oeil*, Barthes wondered if a "psychologie profonde" would not have been more appropriate.[6] Within the subsequent postwar writings of both Sartre and Barthes, however, psychoanalytic considerations will be subordinated to social realities.

Closely identified with the critical essay, Sartre proved to be an important model of the social critic for Barthes. Indeed, the general revitalization of the essay in the fifties responded to several exigencies, including the need for an active participation of intellectuals in the reconstruction of a morally and socially, as well as economically, devastated nation. With the publication of *Writing Degree Zero* in 1953, Barthes's category of *scriptor* reflected the historical change in the function and status of the postwar intellectual:

> The spreading influence of social and political facts into the literary
> field of consciousness has produced a new type of *scriptor*, situated
> midway between party member and the writer, deriving from the first
> an idealized image of the committed man, and from the second the idea
> that a written work is an act. (*Writing Degree Zero*, 26)

Moreover, the strong postwar push for modernization and the inevitable disruptions in collective life brought about by the technological imperative correlate with the appearance of a new scholar—the quantitatively oriented sociologist. The prestige of American social science helped undermine the French university tradition demanding lifetime preparation of a magnum opus and instead encouraged the production and dissemination of information by means of the journal article. Even literary figures felt the impact of a pervasive bias toward a form of essay appropriate to the mode of intervention increasingly favored by Barthes who, along with Bataille and Blanchot, set up other rules and other formulae, for which the essay, article, and fragment are often the new form and new norm. Within this innovative appreciation of time and space, the format and unity of the book seek to recreate the connections otherwise dispersed among separate pieces: the book, during this period, is often a collection of articles, and the journal plays a considerable role in the elaboration and diffusion of knowledge.[7]

Certainly the format of the essay – shorter than a philosophical treatise yet requiring an analytic framework for its political or ethical *prises de position* – provided the ideal conduit for the opinions of writers previously associated with primarily literary pursuits. Furthermore, these essays appeared in journals or reviews founded by an *équipe* whose sense of common purpose and mutual cooperation sustained a sense of community. Thus, while one finds essays by Leiris on racism and colonialism in Sartre's *Les Temps modernes*, Bataille, founder and editor-in-chief of *Critique*, was expounding on the Marshall Plan as a form of gift-giving within the new international economic order, and Barthes was chronicling the first phase of the transformation of *la vieille France* into a consumer society via its "mythologies."

But whereas comparisons with Sartre and Bataille help to situate the Barthesian essay historically, they do not explain its specificity. This is the task undertaken by *The Barthes Effect*. Unlike the essays of Bataille which present an intentional mixture of discourses, the final texts by Barthes concentrate on revising the reader/writer distinction. To the anxiety of Bataille, who feared his eclecticism was so general as to be of relevance to all and of interest to none, Barthes responds with the formation of a new reading space. For Bensmaïa, the utopian text not only puts into motion linguistic antagonisms, but also enjoins the reader to remain "mobile and plural," so as to be able to write along with it. Such a process is possible because of the relinquishment of traditional analysis (including philosophical disquisitions), the rejection of a conventional economy of the subject, and the reconsideration of the classical category of thought. In their place, the reflective text offers a dramaturgical staging of ideas whose effects draw the reader into a recognition scene from which she or he must be distanced. Thus the scriptural equivalent of a Brechtian *Entfremdungseffekt* compels the reader/subject to move beyond the mirror stage in order to play out simulacra of alternative programs or projects. The reinvention of the text-essay, according to Bensmaïa, "is by nature made to provoke in you that which is most regressive, at the same time that it liberates experiences in you that no other type of writing or text can offer" (page 65). The essay then functions as a catalyst among readers to form a "société des amis du texte" negatively bonded by the fact that "they have nothing in common but their enemies" (*PT*, 14–15).

Though perhaps overstated, Barthes's observation undoubtedly applies to his own association with the review *Tel Quel*, a tie whose importance was underscored in the 1977 *Lecture*. Indeed, in one of the strongest sections of *The Barthes Effect*, with the Montaignian title "Oh, a Friend" (*O un amy!*), Bensmaïa reminds us of one of Barthes's early comments regarding the role of journals: "When one writes for a journal, it is not so much of the public one is thinking . . . as of the group of editors . . . a sort of collective address closer to a workshop or seminar" ("Résponses," *Tel Quel* 47, 95). Founded in 1960 by Philippe Sollers, *Tel Quel* is acknowledged as having played a central role in the formulation and dissemination of the major issues of contemporary critical thought without prompting the historical study it deserves.[8] Moreover, the *TQ* texts of Barthes, Derrida, Foucault, Kristeva, and Sollers appear in English separately, making it virtually impossible to appreciate the nature of a project that brought them together to publish the *Théorie d'ensemble* under the review's aegis.

Unlike others who have glossed over the *TQ* connection, Bensmaïa considers its part in Barthes's confrontation with the "morality" of the sign. Following the essay's particular logic, Bensmaïa shows how Barthes enlists the utopian text to desediment the unconscious penetration of historically determined signifieds while protecting the signifier from their total domination. But, whereas the "free play of the signifier" has become a post-structuralist slogan, less interest has been granted Barthes's emphasis on the inevitability of historical appurtenance, a point elaborated in his early definition of *écriture*. Concretely, Barthes understood the impossibility of effecting a historical displacement of the signifier in isolation, whence the vital role of the review, where an *écriture* evolves among "friends" who are both writers and readers.

Bensmaïa does well to highlight the ambivalence of Barthes's position: friendship offers a privileged field of possibilities, that is, "a space where I can escape images, where I can evolve without having to repeatedly justify the words that I use, the tastes that I have, the values that I privilege." But friends are also the group to whom "I yield myself, given the inescapability of alienation" (*PRB*, 308). Just as Barthes argued that the historical determination of *écriture* seriously curtailed the Sartrean ideal of freedom, given that the writer can exert only limited control over the discursive effects of her or his writing, so does the shift from *corpus* to *corps* in the later Barthes carry the problematic of writing to the most intimate details of the body. Subject to the same appropriations as any written text, the body is viewed as a compendium of already-written citations. The question of the morality of the sign is, therefore, especially pertinent. Once he concedes the power of all other determinants—family, milieu, education, discourse—Barthes then wonders whether the body can be depended upon as a privileged site of resistance. More pointedly, he asks, can there be a thought that emanates from the body?

Having mapped out the topology of Barthes's preoccupation with friendship, Bensmaïa traces the network of friends, especially those working on the same journal, to moral positions, making friendship the "ethico-political" problem par excellence. Unable to adequately theorize the concept of morality at stake here (*"une moralité sans morale"*), Barthes also left in abeyance, or at least in abstract terms, the nature of the bond generated by friendship. The somewhat overworked notion of desire (to which he had earlier contrasted a sense of pleasure or *jouissance*) is of little assistance since it only repeats the old question, "Where am I among my desires?" (*RB*, 64).

Given the important insights Bensmaïa provides by linking the body as historical phenomenon to writing and friendship, I would argue that it is now possible to consider how the body as *mot-mana* not only holds together the fragments of Barthes's later texts, but signals a connection among the various Barthes as well. The latter correspond to periodizations which differ among critics who nonetheless all claim a discontinuity between the early and late writings. Unfortunately, the rationales provided by Barthes explaining such shifts tend to be overlooked, as when he criticized his mythologies for being overly formulaic demystifications, dependent on an upending procedure that led to predictable imitations. Yet, subsequent changes in his orientation did not imply a repudiation of their ideological thrust. Certainly the most intimidating obstacle to writing about Barthes, especially if one attempts to treat the work as a whole, comes from the preemptive force of his own self-criticisms. In his war against that "monster" of language dormant in every sign—the stereotype—Barthes scrupulously purged his discourse of the ready-made thoughts that pollute the writing of even the greatest authors. Only to discover their presence within: "Frequently he starts from the stereotype, from the banal opinion, which is in him" (*RB*, 162). The realization that the body is "historical," i.e., social and cultural, and therefore subject to the same appropriative power of discourse as the mind, explains why, inevitably, the final object of analysis for Roland Barthes was himself.

Barthes's confrontations with the historical dimension of the body are scattered throughout *Roland Barthes by Roland Barthes* and, as in *Mythologies*, are often sparked by a verbal expression found in everyday life. One such bittersweet epiphany occurs when, plagued by headaches, he uses the word migraine to describe his *maux de tete*. The linguistic difference between the two, he reflects, is socially based: the first, reserved for the discourse of the "man of letters" and the *"dame bourgeoise,"* signals their distance from the person who spontaneously employs "headaches." Even at this level of detail, Barthes ruefully notes, "Social division occurs within my body: even my body is social" (*RB*, 124).

On another occasion, a simple exchange with the *boulangère* regarding the weather—*"le temps qu'il fait"*—exposes the fiction of social solidarity such banalities are supposed to consolidate. Unlike the case of Dominici (*Mythologies*, 50–53), however, where class conflict was mirrored in grammatical usage, communication breaks down, in this instance, at the more elusive level of the senses:

"I realize that *seeing the light* relates to a class sensibility" (*RB*, 176). Such revelations are ambivalent in their ability to heighten an awareness of self while deepening the distance from the social other. Comparable to Proust's observation that "Françoise remained indifferent to the chirping of the birds," without its wrenching disappointment at missed intimacy, Barthes fills his perception of the gap separating R. B. from his interlocutor with sociological observations, "In short, there is nothing more cultural than the atmosphere, nothing more ideological than what the weather is doing" (*RB*,176).

Barthes's "*moments* im*parfaits*" in many ways assume the three thousand pages of a *recherche* that has become the impossible luxury of a past surviving only in the historical density of the sign "literature." Is not the essay condemned to being *only* an essay in part because it must explain, i.e., analyze, in three sentences that which Proust could indulgently explore in the *jouissance* of an *écriture* subject to the economy of another era? To what extent does the Barthesian essay bear witness to the fact that the great social frescoes of the last century, culminating in the Proustian monument, have been superseded by the "sciences of man?" Conversely, one could argue that much recent French sociology (viz. Bourdieu) often seems little more than a footnote to Proust. Indeed, few modern writers have understood better than Barthes the shift in the model of class conflict from the production of goods in the nineteenth century to the production of signs in the twentieth. The locus of power is no longer ownership but *access* to and control over the codes governing information, understood in the broad sense of all sign-systems. Sociologists of postindustrial culture point out that the dividing lines are no longer drawn in terms of exploitation, but between those who dominate and those who are so dominated. These assumptions are fundamental to Barthes's understanding of language, ideology, and politics. As his career progressed, he undoubtedly expanded his revulsion against bourgeois mental habits to all manifestations of closure, whether emanating from right or left. The refusal to privilege any one discourse as somehow immune to the egregious invasions of the cliché contributed to the impression of a progressively more apolitical aestheticism, or, in his own terms, the triumph of *écriture* over analysis. But only *écriture* both undoes the barriers of social difference and formulates alternative languages, so that it must be appreciated as the nemesis of writing-as-instrument, the unreflective transcription of the *doxa* or "that which goes without saying."

By approaching the politics of writing "diagonally," Bensmaïa provides the reader with the most appropriate basis on which to consider an issue found throughout the essays but surfacing in various guises. It is therefore not surprising that some of the most serious consequences of Barthes's having connected language, friendship, and the morality of the sign to the body, are reconsidered in those sections dealing with his ties to a journal.

In a recent "*mémoire*," Julia Kristeva situates the place of *Tel Quel* within her own affective, intellectual trajectory in ways that are pertinent to Barthes.[9] First, her hyperbolic description of language helps us to appreciate its exceptional prestige and full implications within a certain discourse: "When thought concedes its debt to language—and that is the case, well before structuralism, within the French essayistic tradition—the speaking subject is thrown into Infinity conceived as the power and ruse of the Word." Second, she reminds us that *Tel Quel* provided a privileged link to post-structuralism at a time when the impact of structuralism "tilted toward an analysis of subjectivity, leading to the formation of a new theoretical discourse on language viewed as a subjective experience." The classical notion of the subject is thus reconsidered within the possibilities of an innovative theoretical framework. Moreover, in the early *Tel Quel* texts, such proposals were forwarded in the name of a cultural revolution. Whence yet another dimension of Barthes's ambivalence regarding the ability of the *TQ* group to speak a common language; namely, a political language that R. B., the recalcitrant political subject, finds it *viscerally* impossible to enounce: "My body cannot accommodate itself to generality, to the power of generality which is in language" (*RB*,175).

Of course, generality is what guarantees communication, although it exacts the sacrifice of singularity. Barthes must again turn to the body as site of resistance, only to concede to an embarrassingly anachronistic *sensibilité* more responsive to the amenities of a nineteenth-century bourgeois life-style than to the Maoism of his contemporaries. As counterpoint to the two transgressive "Goddesses" (hashish and homosexuality) by which he might be identified, Barthes divulges the source of the "contretemps," to which his inner rhythms seem to really beat— the metronome of the *jeune fille bourgeoise*! (*RB*,52). Haunting the *Roland Barthes* is a *demoiselle* playing the piano while Paris burned in '68. Faced with the inescapability of *la condition bourgeoise*, Barthes compromised on a utopian fantasy reconciling a Proustian afternoon tea with the equality of a socialist society (*RB*,60).

The perspective of the poetician forwarded in Bensmaïa's excellent study underscores *écriture*'s "aphoristic energy" (Derrida) as an effective subverter of the law of genre. Nonetheless committed to distinguishing the later texts, Bensmaïa identifies them in part by the anxiety Barthes experienced at the desire for a sense of identity in light of the gnawing question, "What is the value of a thought constrained only by the words of the tribe?" Resisting the temptation to impose closure on the questions raised by the final fragments, Bensmaïa responds with intertextual reference to the Nietzschean semiology of self, as read through Pierre Klossowski's study. According to *Nietzsche et le cercle vicieux*, the individual's only defense against the "institutional significance given by the gregarious group"[10] is through simulacra. And Bensmaïa reminds us that such phantasmatic simulation leads to images.

The ambivalence traced thus far is carried through to the very last writings, where the tension between the security of language within its exchange-value and the imperatives of singularity, with its risk of a descent into mutism or insanity, now acquires a greater dramatic significance. The "inner oscillations" (a description borrowed from Nietzsche) driving Barthes between the social space of friendship and the unmediated haven of the mother become intolerable following her death. Moreover, the intellectualized attempt to "speak his particularity" takes on a new urgency with the passing of the only person capable of ensuring it. In *Camera Lucida* Barthes exhausts his torment in a paroxysm of Pity. Encountering the "love" elicited by certain photographs, the writer tells how

> another music is heard, its name oddly old-fashioned. Pity. I collected
> in a last thought the images which had "pricked" me. . . . In each of
> them, inescapably . . . I entered crazily into the spectacle, into the im-
> age, taking into my arms what is dead, what is going to die, as
> Nietzsche did when on January 3, 1889, he threw himself in tears on
> the neck of a beaten horse: gone mad for Pity's sake. (*CL*, 116–117)

Has Barthes abandoned the reflective text for the transparency of a maternal *regard*? Rather than Nietzsche, perhaps the apt reference here is Rousseau, for whom Pity – the cornerstone of an egalitarian anthropology – is an eminently presocial sentiment, relating individuals not yet subject to the laws of difference.

Following this juxtaposition of extraordinary images, Bensmaïa returns to the question of the Barthesian essay in relation to all those possible categorizations it systematically eludes. Barthes himself noted that the task of poetics is not to ascribe meaning, but to consider how it is produced. With admirable tact and sensitivity, Bensmaïa navigates between theoretical issues and the motif of the body as it travels into the most personal details of the Barthesian *corp(u)s*. As promised, he guides the reader through the vagaries of an *écriture* whose charms and challenges critics before him were tempted to dismiss as Parisian chic. With appropriate deference, he considers Barthes one of the foremost theoreticians of literature of his generation, without artificially constructing from the fragmentary pieces a discourse, system, or science in conformity with traditional standards.

To what extent does *The Barthes Effect* resolve the opening enigma of Barthes's self-critical appraisal? From one perspective, it helps us appreciate the paradox of the essay as "only" an essay precisely because it is an open-ended, interminable writing machine. As the French are etymologically reminded, it constantly tries out new ways, with the result that it is always on trial. To the extent that the term is still applicable, the essay, as Bensmaïa provocatively argues, must therefore not be appreciated as *a* genre, but the one from which all others are generated.

This sense of renewal or, more accurately, of nostalgic beginnings, imbues one of Barthes's very last lessons, placed under the Proustian heading "*longtemps, je me suis couché de bonne heure.*"[11] Following by a year the lecture cited above, this address explores with even greater poignancy the desire to write caught between the critical exigencies of the essay and the affective pull of the novel. Without laboring the obvious parallels to his own history, Barthes notes that *La Recherche* was preceded by a considerable number of essays and initiated only after the death of Proust's mother. As a third way or alternative to the unsatisfying options dictated by genre convention, it reveals a meeting of the two paths the narrator also learns ultimately do meet. Similarly, Barthes fantasizes an as yet unrealized form inspired by the "bad" sleep of the *Recherche*'s deviations from linear narrative. Comparing the musicality of Proust's work to a "rhapsodic" structure, or to a gown that the dressmaker submits "to crisscrossings, to arrangements, to repetitions," he elevates the dress to an original art form, irreducible to mere patchwork. The cross-references to Proust renew ties with the Baudelairean "spirituality" of clothing, while the embellished *tissu* of Barthes's own *écriture* allows him to figuratively recover from the vulnerability of self-exposure.

Further on, the description of Proust's work as a "sumptuous effort" highlights the embeddedness of theoretical concerns within the exquisite detail of this writing. Barthes's oxymoron defies the rationality of a civilization that opposes work to art, production to eroticism, and *savoir* to *saveur*. Excessive refinement in both Proust and Barthes, however, only thinly veils their respective dances with death: The special intimacy Barthes now seeks is prefigured in the pained query *"Quel Lucifer a crée en même temps l'amour et la mort?"* by pointing to the biographical sources of the literature he admires most.

The importance of the sumptuous effort of the *Recherche* is that it distinguishes remembered time from the "false permanences" of the biography. Conversely, I have argued against the artificial breaks of critical periodization. Not that Barthes's plea for new beginnings should not be respected, even when as here, they take up old, i.e., false antinomies. From Dante's *Vita Nuova* he learned that the innovative path leads to a new writing practice. Despite the counterforces of generality and science, it was capable of identifying an intimate self, the one "for which there is no substitute." Following an equally circuitous trajectory, Derrida also returns to literature or "that thing" it seems to welcome better than philosophy. After twenty years of transgressing the law of genre in search of an idiom whose special economy "possesses a property that we cannot appropriate," he still dreams of

> a language or song that must be one's own, though not identified by the attributes of a "self", but by the musicality of an invisible history. I am not referring to a style, but to an intersection of singularities, habits, voices, traces – what moves with you and never leaves your body.[12]

Are we to infer that for Barthes fulfillment is now equated with writing a novel? Does this signal a definitive break with the predominantly intellectual nature of preceding works ("even if novelistic elements disrupt their rigor"?). More enticing than the actual execution of such a work is its very possibility. The hypothetical *Vita Nuova* will be completed by a *Scienza Nuova*, since it is from the encounter of the two that his fanciful third way emerges. Barthes's ambivalence now garners a new dimension, given that the force of his writing embraces what is normally separate, opposite, or even irreconcilable. Like Proust, he refuses to be a divided subject, so that the essay's metaphorical "what is it?" cannot be separated from narrative's metonymical "what next?" The latter spurs the reader to continue while the first assures analytic repose. Master of rhetoric, Barthes will not sacrifice either axis of writing. He also understood that the elusive identity of the writing self ultimately resides with the reader. So in this last call for renewal, he concludes with a question: ostensibly, it solicits a response; in reality, it leads to the next text, as well as all others, both past and future:

> Perhaps it is at the heart of this subjectivity, of this intimacy with which I engaged you, that I am scientific without knowing it, confusedly turned toward the *Scienza Nuova* of which Vico spoke: ought it not express both the brilliance and the suffering of the world, that which both seduces me and arouses my indignation?[13]

Until Barthes, the essay may have been only an essay. He made it much more.

Preface

This text reproduces in part, with some important changes, a doctoral dissertation prepared under the direction of Gérard Genette and defended at the Ecole Pratique des Hautes Etudes en Sciences Sociales in Paris. I have made substantial additions – including all of the section entitled "Oh, a Friend!" – and I have reworked everything that pertains to the notion of "reflective text," which I did not elaborate until after the defense of my thesis. These pages bear the mark of their origin: resulting from my doctoral studies, they have a didactic purpose and make liberal use of quotations and illustrations to support my arguments.

This work deals with the rhetorical analysis of the Essay as a "genre"; it does not claim to be exhaustive. It is not meant to be, for example, a study of Barthes's "thought." That would have been a much more ambitious project than this modest contribution to the understanding of a practice of writing (*écriture*) that up to now has not had the attention it deserves.

In any case, I am not unaware that by taking on what I shall call the "late" work of Barthes, my reading presupposes a certain "evolution" – or, to put it in the terms that Stephen Heath formulated expressly to discuss Barthes, certain "displacements" that require a theoretical "explanation." In the final section of this book, I have attempted to (at least) sketch what seems to me to have determined both the remodeling of semiology deemed necessary by Barthes and its practical and poetical consequences. Barthes is not one of those writers of whom it can be said (for reassurance) that they have *one* thought. The critical reader cannot capture Barthes in the form of a digest – cannot, that is to say, divide him into periods each representing a step in the perfection of his thought. "Tactics without strategy," Barthesian writing and thought follow instead a logic that we will connect more easily with the Nietzschean eternal return than with the dialectic of Hegelian or Marxian phenomenology. This explains why the post-structuralist Barthes can be found in the deceptively positivist Barthes of *Mythologies* or *The Fashion System*. Because my interest lies primarily in Barthes the poetician and writer, my approach perhaps did not consider in sufficient detail the stages through which Barthes passed to arrive at *A Lover's Discourse* or *Roland Barthes by Roland Barthes*. Nevertheless, I hope that emphasizing certain of the effects that Barthes expected from the writing he so well defined and practiced will better clarify the "structural" viewpoint that I have adopted here. Bergson has said that in every real author one can find a fundamental "intuition" that does not explain the work but at least serves as a guiding thread. Instead of following an idea, I followed a word—the "mana-word" *body*—and I saw things *seemingly* fall into place *by themselves*. In rereading the inaugural lecture that Barthes gave at the Collège de France, I am again struck by the extraordinary weight Barthes gives to the body—his body: Does the body really have a story? Is the body subject to an evolution *once and for all*? If the answer is no, what happens to the text? To writing? To literature? To his beloved? In short—and this is related to what I have just said—I did not think it useful to retrace the different stages through which Barthes passed before giving way to what Blanchot would call "fragmentary exigency." This is not a purely descriptive study; it is meant to shed light on the question of fragmentation in the Barthesian text and thus to facilitate the comprehension of Barthes's works both ideologically and poetically.

I would like to end—and not merely for the sake of convention—by thanking those without whose support this work would not have been possible. I am especially grateful to Joëlle Proust, who discussed this work with me step-by-step and helped me to progress and to smooth out the difficulties; to Gérard Genette, who read the work at various stages and whose critical comments helped me to deepen my approach to the work of the "later" Barthes; to Wlad Godzich of the University of Minnesota and the Université de Montréal, who read the first drafts of my book and encouraged me to undertake further elaboration; to Denis Hollier of the University of California at Berkeley, and Michèle Richman of the University of Pennsylvania, who in various ways applied their critical acumen to my manuscript and helped me to give it its present form; to Tom Conley, who believed in this work and accepted one of the chapters in the journal that he edits at the University of Minnesota; to Marie-Hélène Huet, to whom I owe the title of my book as well as invaluable encouragement; to Jacqueline Leiner, who was kind enough to read the manuscript and suggest changes; and to Jacques Demougin, who has asked to include a part of my text—the Appendix—in the first volume of the *Larousse de la Littérature*. I would also like to thank Jean-François Lyotard and Louis Marin, who helped me during the writing of my dissertation with their friendly criticism and encouragement. I thank, too, Eileen Sivert, Pat Fedkiew, and Kate Brady, all of the University of Minnesota, whose invaluable help, rendered in various capacities, made possible the English version of my manuscript. Finally, I want to thank the Graduate School at the University of Minnesota for the grant I received for the translation of this text.

R. B.

Introduction
The "Reflective" Text

What calls forth the act of writing when a book's time, determined by the relationship of the beginning to the end, and when a book's space, determined by the deployment about a center, are no longer imperative?

(Maurice Blanchot, L'Entretien infini, *625)*

Can one identify a work of art, of whatever sort, but especially a work of discursive art, if it does not bear the mark of a genre, if it does not signal or mention it or make it remarkable in any way?

(Jacques Derrida, "The Law of Genre," Glyph *7, 211)*

All method is a fiction. Language has appeared as the instrument of fiction; it will follow the method of language, language reflecting upon itself.

(Stéphane Mallarmé)[1]

The writerly is the novelistic without the novel, poetry without the poem, the essay without the dissertation, writing without style, production without product, structuration without structure.

(S/Z, 5)

The intrusion, into the discourse of the essay, of a third person who nonetheless refers to no fictive creature, marks the necessity of remodeling the genres: let the essay avow itself almost *a novel: a novel without proper names.*

(RB, *120*)

It is not easy to write about the work of Roland Barthes. One reason is that Barthes has always in some way accompanied his texts with his own anticipated commentary; consequently, to talk or write about Barthes is necessarily, to some extent, to repeat him, quote him, or betray him.[2] Another reason is that the "object," "method," and "ideology" of his work have always been subjected to a perpetual displacement.

Indeed, as Gérard Genette remarks in *Figures I* [3], from *Writing Degree Zero* (1953) to the *Critical Essays* (1966) Barthes passed through almost every trend that dominated the literary scene, going from existentialism to structuralism after having practiced and given new vigor to the "psychoanalysis of substances," Marxism, and both Freudian and Lacanian psychoanalysis—without ever permitting himself to be linked exclusively or definitively to any of these.

In retrospect, I see Barthes's work as constituted essentially of mutations and ruptures which resist all efforts at synthesis or recovery. Like the *Mana* of Claude Lévi-Strauss, Barthes's text is "neither eccentric nor central; it is motionless and carried, floating, never *pigeonholed*, always atopic (escaping any topic), at once remainder and supplement, a signifier taking up the place of every signified" (*RB*, 129).

It is nonetheless true, however, that in spite of its "apparent eclecticism" (Genette, ibid., 186) and lack of "unity," Barthes's oeuvre has always seemed animated by a secret ambition: to bring together in one writing movement, in a single *Text*, modes of discourse that had hitherto been kept separate—that of the *écrivain* and that of the *écrivant* and also that of the "producer" (the Author) of the text and its "user."[4] Texts of the last period like *The Pleasure of the Text* and *A Lover's Discourse*, and especially *Roland Barthes by Roland Barthes* and *Camera Lucida*, inaugurate, in this sense, a new way of investigating and interrogating *literature*, that supposedly homogeneous entity. They also introduce a new "style" or type of writing that is certainly closer to the Montaignian essay than to the kind of "critical" essay that Sartre was still seeking to define and renew in the 1950s.[5]

What I would like to bring to the fore in this book is that by turning once more to *the* Genre of the Essay—by "polishing up" as he says, "the great book" (*RB*, 173)—Barthes does not simply *change genres or registers*; he engages in a sort of *generalized repetition* (*répétition générale*) of the movement that, from Montaigne's *Essays* to Maurice Blanchot's *L'Entretien infini* by way of the German Romantics, had sedulously contested the validity of reigning theories of genres.[6]

By setting out to write fragments, then, Barthes not only changes his mode of writing; he finds in this change a means—a "tactic"—that enables him to put to literature the most radical question possible: not about its "essence"—literature "in general" does not exist for the Barthesian essayist—but about its Law.[7] Specifically, such a question as: "Why is there Genre, and not Literature instead?"[8]

By committing himself to the fragment, Barthes endows his writing with a note of challenge: for, once a fragmental text is possible, what significance can be attributed to the "resistance" and persistence of *the* Genres bequeathed us by the History of Literature—the "literary institution" (*S/Z*, 4)? Barthes's interest in the *economy* of the fragmental text—of the *Text*—seems to be totally linked to a tactic that aims to demonstrate that the fragmental text not only is possible, but is the "matrix" of all genres. It is not the "Mélange of genres" but the genre of self-generation.[9]

In this perspective, an essay like *S/Z* should no longer be read as merely another of Barthes's texts but as a book that marks a *turning-point*, a privileged instrument of the critical "rehearsal" I spoke of above. Contrary to appearances, *S/Z* is not a *thetic* text or an *alethic* text; it does not seek to establish any principle or affirm any truth concerning literature in general. It is a *programmatic* text that sketches out—"*en creux*" (in intaglio), as Barthes puts it, or "in theory"—the "book to come"—that is, in the Barthesian terminology of *S/Z*, the *writerly* text.[10] My working hypothesis is the following: in proposing the categories of writerly and/or readerly text(s) and in deconstructing the canonical categories of reading and writing, (textual) production and consumption, producer and user—and also those of Novelistic and Novel, Poetry and Poem, writing and style, structuration and structure, and others—Barthes, in a certain sense, was giving the "program" of his works to come. In this sense, *S/Z* can be read as an anticipated *commentary* on the "ideal text" that Barthes was to put into practice systematically and consistently following the publication of *S/Z*.

As we know, Barthes defined this ideal text as follows:

> This text is a galaxy of signifiers, not a structure of signifieds; it has no beginning; it is reversible; we gain access to it by several entrances, none of which can be authoritatively declared to be the main one; the codes it mobilizes extend *as far as the eye can reach*; they are indeterminable (meaning here is never subject to a principle of determination, unless by throwing dice); the systems of meaning can take over this absolutely plural text, but their number is never closed, based as it is on the infinity of language. (*S/Z*, 5–6)

By writing—hard on the heels of *S/Z* and in rapid succession—*The Pleasure of the Text*, *A Lover's Discourse*, *Roland Barthes by Roland Barthes*, and *Camera Lucida*, each very much the same sort of "propadeutic to all future modern texts" as *S/Z*, Barthes will achieve, in a way, this "program" of writing: texts that are, in Barthes's own terms, "plural" and "broken" (lacking "deep structure" and purely "tactical"), constructed from non-totalizable fragments and from exuberantly proliferating "details," calling upon an "economy" of reading and text that I intend to bring to the fore in this study.

Indeed, from a certain perspective all the texts of the latter period can be interpreted and read as the "reversion" of the program of reading and writing opened by the category of *writerly* insofar as it subverts all the anti-thetic instances governing the production and "consumption" of the "readerly" text.

In the paragraph entitled "Step by Step" (*S/Z*, 11–13), Barthes gives us a sketch of this program. If we want to remain attentive to the "plural of a text," he says, we must (1) renounce structuring the text to be read (to be written) *in large masses*, according to the principles of rhetorical *compositio*: "Everything signifies ceaselessly and several times, but without being delegated to a great final ensemble, to an ultimate structure"; (2) study, analyze this "single text" "down to the last detail," by working back along "the threads of meanings"; (3) substitute for the "representative model" "another model" that would avoid "penetrating, reversing the tutor text, giving an internal image of it": "the *step-by-step* method . . . is never anything but the *decomposition* (in the cinematographic sense) of the work of reading: a *slow motion*, so to speak, neither wholly image nor wholly analysis"; (4) and, finally, we must "systematically use digression."

In writing his late essays, Barthes systematically applies each of the principles in this program; only this time, not to the *reading* of a text, but to the *production* and *writing* of a *single* text. In other words, it seems as if, in writing *The Pleasure of the Text*, *A Lover's Discourse*, *Roland Barthes by Roland Barthes* and *Camera Lucida*, Barthes, determined to bring about a "reversion" or "mutation" of the text, has definitively renounced *criticism*. Henceforth, it is less a matter of interpreting the beloved text so as to produce its meaning than of *writing* a new text from non-totalizable fragments – those which the reader of the text isolates "at the very moment of his bliss" (*PT*, 7). From now on, this "undertaking" appears as a complex operation that includes (at least) three distinct moments: (1) producing a text that, right from the start, will be a "galaxy of signifiers," instead of working back along "the threads of meanings"; (2) proceeding directly to the "decomposition" of every text (this being the "work" of reading), instead of producing a (new) model (of the text) or substituting one model for another; (3) finally, systematically using digression to produce a text that abolishes the "distance" that until now has separated the producer of the text from its consumer, instead of preparing a commentary. Therefore, it is no surprise that this text, essentially based on the abolition of the paradigmatic slash mark separating the reader of the text from the writer, presents itself at first as an "impossible" text. Renouncing both (philosophical) "system" and rhetorical composition, this text belongs to no generic category. Nevertheless, it is *constituted formally*: a *writerly* text – a writing of a reading – it demands that the reader change from simple consumer to producer.

Midway between the "writerly" text—about which, as Barthes says, there "may be nothing to say" and which is "difficult to find in bookstores" (*S/Z*)—and the "readerly" text (whose "pluralism" is "parsimonious") there is, as I hope to demonstrate, an intermediate category that I will call the *reflective* text:[11] a text that Barthes inaugurates, as it were, with *S/Z* and whose objectives and ambitions are realized in the latter works.

But how is a text of this type—reversible, lacking a beginning, offering a multiplicity of "entrances," mobilizing its codes *as far as the eye can reach*— possible? To put it another way, in what sense can it be said that *The Pleasure of the Text, A Lover's Discourse, Roland Barthes by Roland Barthes*, and *Camera Lucida* are "reflective" texts? First, as "essays" (see the Appendix), these texts *reflect theoretically* on a certain number of problems and "classical" literary themes—story, structure, reading, writing, narrative, and so on—and, at this level, appear as *transparent* texts: they may be read as simple texts of *criticism* whose theses can be *enumerated* and *discussed*, whose rhetoric (these are the texts of "*écrivants*," not "*écrivains*") can be *qualified*, and whose deployment of the various terminologies that they mobilize (Marxist, structuralist, psychoanalytic, etc.) can be situated. Thus, the "obedient, conformist, plagiarizing" *edge* (*PT*, 6) characterizing these texts; the provisional concession that they make to literary "science" and "theory": a science, a theory that, for Barthes, as we know, cannot really serve to establish a typology of "value" for "modern" texts since their objective is above all the production of an in-different "copy" or "model" that precludes the singularity of the text and "reduces" its plurality.

Second, because these are at the same time texts that no longer "reflect" or are the reflection of a "value of representation"—Cause, Origin, Meaning, Model, etc.—as produced by an "ideological" reading (*S/Z*); on the contrary, they reflect a *practice of writing* that no longer cheats the reader: "Doom of the essay, compared to the novel: doomed to *authenticity*—to the preclusion of quotation marks" (*RB*, 89). But as "reflective" texts, Barthes's essays no longer *comment*, they *write* and move their reader to action; they no longer question the meaning of literary "works" but are a practical interrogation of reading and writing, or more exactly of literature as a product of a writing/reading, of a "lexeography," in Barthesian terms. To describe the genre of text under consideration here, we could take verbatim what Barthes says concerning the "writerly" text: "It is *ourselves writing*, before the infinite play of the world (the world as function) is traversed, intersected, stopped, plasticized by some singular system (Ideology, Genus, Criticism)" (*S/Z*, 5).

In my estimation, there are at least two ways to read *S/Z* and consequently the texts it announces and, in a certain way, makes *possible* and *necessary*. It can be read as a *theoretical* (reflexive) text—another one—on literature, narration, form, and the like. It can also be read as a "reflective" text, a text that has transgressed the paradigmatic slash mark—the "pitiless divorce," as Barthes says—that the "literary institution" maintains between the producer of the text and its user (*S/Z*, 4), between the literary text and the "critical" text.[12]

What I am undertaking here is neither a commentary nor an analysis of certain *theses* in *S/Z*, nor yet a comprehensive interpretation of Barthes's work—we shall see that his work would not withstand this—but rather what I might call a turning of the text, turning it over and about like a mirror or, to offer a more accurate metaphor, turning about the text as if it were an anamorphosis, thus prompting the appearance not of its signified but of its transversal reflection—what it reflects "obliquely," as Montaigne would say.

In proposing to study the rhetorico-formal economy of the essay as a "reflective text," I am not taking up the work of a *historian* of literature so much as that of a "poetician": by opening this book with a study of the essay that Montaigne bequeathed to posterity, I intend not so much to insist on the nature of the ties connecting Montaigne to Barthes,[13] as to shed light on the systematic and transindividual character of traits present in each of them. Moreover, the works of Barthes himself led me in this direction. Didn't he, in an especially programmatic text, write that "if through a twisted dialectic, the Text, destroyer of all subject, contains a subject to love, that subject is dispersed, somewhat like the ashes we strew into the wind after death" (*SFL*, 8–9)? These "ashes"—the dissemination of those "tastes," "details," and "inflections"[14] that constitute the "charm" and determine the efficacy of Barthes's later texts—are already functioning in Montaigne.

As we know, it is a long tradition by now that has handed down to us a Montaigne who is viewed as an "author" of essays and creator of a genre in which caprice, improvisation, and the arbitrary and impulsive ("irresponsible") linking of ideas seem to be the rule. Of all the works that have a place in the history of literature, the *Essays* were long considered—and this view still persists here and there—the freest and the most difficult to reduce to the accepted norms of Rhetoric. The image of a Montaigne unable to control his subject or too prolix and confusedly organizing his material (Pascal, Fortunat Strowski), haphazardly throwing together his work (Pierre Champion), or not having found *the* appropriate form with which to present his ideas (Gide), has become indissociable from the *Essays*. Now, I would like to show—by beginning with Montaigne and returning to him through what will be found in Barthes's work—that it is not at all fortuitous or accidental that the notions of incompletion and inexhaustibility have been associated with Montaigne's *Essays* and through them with the Essay as a specific genre. In fact, historians of literature and poeticians of the genres have failed to classify the Essay satisfactorily or to recognize its originality precisely because they have historically assimilated the functioning of *all* literary work to the "rhetorical synthesis of its presentation." Because the operatory and functional character of all *possible* texts was identified with certain rhetorical and logical norms of exposition, or with certain "philosophical" criteria for the treatment and presentation of Ideas,[15] the form of the Essay as a specific genre was to remain unanalyzed for a long time and the particular nature of its efficacy was to remain a mystery. Now, even if the form is no longer, as it was for Valéry the essayist, a "means of controlling the mobility [and] inconstancy of the mind"—in other words, even if it undertakes the inverse of the Valérian "program" and becomes an efficacious means to *realize and implement* the mind's "mobility" and "inconstancy"—work in the essay form clearly implies a notion of construction and calculation (of a "tactic," as Barthes puts it) "that one must [continue to] distinguish from any idea of completion or, more generally, of the constructed presentation."[16] That is to say, our long-standing difficulty in accounting for what takes place in the *Essays* stems less from the disparity, the heterogeneity, or the dispersion of parts or themes—the multiplicity of "suppositions," as Hugo Friedrich puts it—than from our inability to learn a certain mode of *reading* with its concomitant expectations. By studying the arrangement and functioning of the late essays of Barthes after those of Montaigne, I propose a sort of apprenticeship: an apprenticeship in a new mode of reading the texts of modernity—of reading their "genre."

The Barthes Effect

The Barthes Effect

1. The Logic of the "Sufficient Word" in the Montaignian Essay

For a long time it was assumed that only with the *Essays* of *Book III* did Montaigne find his definitive style and pinpoint the specific strategy for which he is recognized. Nevertheless, because of Montaigne's continuous rewriting, *Book I* has at least one text where Montaigne proposes, together with a theory of reading, an explanation of the constitutive method of the *Essays*.[1] The following is a fragment from "A Consideration upon Cicero" in which Montaigne sets forth some rudiments of his poetics:

> In order to get more in, *I pile up only the headings of subjects.* Were I to add on their consequences, I *would multiply* this volume *many times over.* And how many stories have I spread around *which say nothing of themselves*, but from which anyone who *troubles to pluck them with a little ingenuity will produce numberless Essays.*
>
> Neither these stories nor my quotations serve always simply for *example, authority*, or *ornament.* I do not esteem them solely for the *use* I derive from them. They often bear, *outside of my subject*, the seeds of a richer and bolder material, and sound obliquely a subtler note, both for myself, who do not wish to express anything more, and for those who get my drift. (I. 40, 185, emphasis mine)[2]

In this text dating from the *first* period of the *Essays*, Montaigne states a fundamental principle of his poetics: corresponding to the *scriptural actuality* of a given essay there is always a *lectural potentiality* irreducible to a "finite" mode

3

of reading or reader. The particular structure of the essay permits the production of an *indefinite* number of developments from a finite set of elements. Therefore, there are always some pieces of story, some fragments of thought, some "bits" of quotation which, even if they do not come to anything in a given essay, even if they do not find the means to deploy their potentialities, will nevertheless continue to work in subterranean fashion. "Consequences" are lacking, there are only "headings" of certain ideas, thoughts, stories, etc. But this in no way precludes the essay from making them produce a maximum meaning. It is only in accordance with the principle of a closed system that a text can be said to be finite. Whoever wants to "pluck with a little ingenuity" a text not subject to any prior rhetorical norm will see that the essay appears *positively*: (*a*) as a potentially infinite and open text; (*b*) as a piling up — the metaphor is constant in Montaigne — or juxtaposition of *n* fragments. As Montaigne writes elsewhere, "I am likely to begin without a plan; the first remark leads to a second. . . . I would rather compose two letters than close and fold one."

When Montaigne specifies that his "quotations" do not serve as "examples," "authority," or "ornament," he clearly indicates their status as fragments: only insofar as they are taken into the general organization of the text — which they populate with a thousand potentialities — and not insofar as they focus on some "philosophical consideration"[3] do fragments, bits, or pieces of stories produce their specific effects. They preserve throughout the mark of their original fragmentation: an arrangement of heterogeneous elements, a mélange or "mixture"[4] of discussion with oneself, of free conversation, of letter or address, and also of sententiae and maxims. The unity of the essayistic text demands a new definition of the notion of text as well as a new position for reading. In fact, since the organizer of the text is no longer a principle of authority — Montaigne is neither the representative of a particular philosophical system nor the exponent of particular philosophical theses or questions — the reader will have to forge a path through the scattered fragments. This explains why the essayist can only reject the stereotyped usage of *exemplum* and quotation: in the essay, they no longer serve as illustration or confirmation of a thesis; rather, they are an element wholly constitutive of what traditionally tends to be hidden in the economy of classical texts: that is to say, their processive aspect — or, if you like, the rhetorical "artifices" that are constantly at work in them.

There is thus a "supernumerary" effect (I will consider this at greater length later) that is inextricably and essentially linked to the method of composition of the essay as text — "seeds of a richer and bolder material," as Montaigne says, that cannot be reduced. A classical point of view, invoking theories of "oblique vision" and "grotesques," would explain his accumulation of examples, stories, and the like as a horror of didacticism and a taste for suggestiveness.[5] This is the sort of explanation found in Michel Butor's book on the *Essays* or in Michaël Baraz's study of the "images" in the *Essays*. Whatever their interest, such analyses do not throw a great deal of light on the nature of the genre, perhaps because they consider it only obliquely. These works lead us to believe that we are dealing still with a mode of composition and of writing in which the author's mastery over the text is the governing factor. But when Montaigne says that his stories and examples go outside his subject, everything points to another type of textual economy: here, marginal effects and the overflow of meaning become the rule.

If we decide to follow Montaigne in renouncing the order, disposition, and canonical closure of the composed text, we can try to account for the mode of functioning of the essay as a "literary machine" (Deleuze) capable of producing, *at the same time*, supernumerary surface effects, subjects that are rash and bold, oblique resonances and "infinite Essays" without *breaking down*. To do so, we must change our point of view and leave off studying the essays as if the form of their exposition and the mode of their functioning were extrinsic. "If I were a professional," Montaigne said, "I would naturalize art as much as they artialize nature."

When one studies the many texts in which Montaigne sets forth the "principles" of his poetics, the striking feature is his insistence on the intrinsic productivity of the form of each one of his *Essays*. This is readily apparent in the celebrated text in *Book III* where Montaigne puts on a dress rehearsal, as it were, of his poetics.

To the question of why he has just taken such a long "detour"—*quo diversibus abis*—on the "dismemberment" of France with its concomitant divisions and difficulties, Montaigne replies:

(1) This stuffing is a bit *outside of my subject*. I wander a little, but *rather by license than carelessness*. My fantasies follow one another, but sometimes it is from a distance, and *look at each other*, but *obliquely*, with a sidelong glance.

(2) I have run my eyes over a certain dialogue of Plato, a fantastic motley in two parts, the beginning part about love, all the rest about rhetoric. The ancients do not fear these changes, and with wonderful grace *they let themselves thus be tossed in the wind, or seem to*. The titles of my chapters do not always embrace their matter; often *they only denote it by some mark*, like those other titles, *The Maid of Andros, The Eunuch*, or those other names, Sulla, Cicero, Torquatus. I love the poetic gait, by leaps and gambols. It is an art, as Plato says, light, flighty, daemonic. There are works of Plutarch's in which *he forgets his theme*, in which the treatment of *his subject is found only incidentally*, quite smothered in foreign matter. See his movements in "The Daemon of Socrates." Lord, *what beauty there is in these lusty sallies and this variation, and more so the more nonchalant and fortuitous they seem*.

(3) *It is the inattentive reader who loses my subject, not I. Some* word about it will always be found off in a corner, which will not fail to be *sufficient* [*bastant*], although it may be concise. I seek out change

indiscriminately and tumultuously. My *style* and my *mind* alike go wandering. (III. 9, 761, emphasis mine)

This text echoes Montaigne's text that was analyzed earlier: all the previously stated poetic principles are reaffirmed, sometimes in the *same terms*. It will be recalled that in the first text, Montaigne concludes by noting (1) that in the logic of his system of exposition, "stories" and "quotations" often go "outside of [his] subject" and bear "the seeds of a richer and bolder material"; and (2) that between these stories and quotations there sounds a "subtler note," a resonance that should be taken into consideration. In the latter text the same problems provide the impetus for his poetic reflection. It is as if poetics, too, demands the same system of resumptions and resonances as that necessary for the smooth functioning of the essay as reflective text. In repeating himself, Montaigne shows that he is conscious of the rhetorical difficulties raised by his text. And this time the new metaphors lead us to an essential point: What is the logic that allows the fragments, in spite of their extreme heterogeneity, to constitute a *unity*?

In the first sequence of Montaigne's text quoted above, this unity is described as the *resonance* of a series of stories: there is a unity of "fantasies," but it is "oblique," transverse. What may appear as wandering—a total lack of order—is in fact an *exigency* characteristic of essayistic writing. The second sequence develops this theme by invoking Plato and Plutarch, very freely interpreted. Montaigne focuses, in a sense, on the aporetic and—in certain aspects—"polyphonic" side of Plato's early dialogues[6] in order to reaffirm a characteristic I have mentioned earlier: the *Essays* open dialogue form. But he also takes up an aspect of Plutarch's *Moral Works*—providentially devoted to Socrates' daemon—in order to be more specific. In the first sequence, Montaigne has said: "My fantasies follow one other, but sometimes it is from a distance, and look at each other, but obliquely"; relying on Plutarch, he specifies that the "subjects" are produced only *incidentally*. Definite *intention* and *plan* do not guide and punctuate the scansion of what the essay proposes; rather, the multiplicity and initial heterogeneity of the elements of the work determine the appearance of particular utterances.[7] Thus what matters to the essayist is not the classical question of rhetorical *inventio*— finding something to say—nor that of *dispositio*—putting in order what has been found.[8] Rather it is a problem of *complicatio*, which consists in producing, as Barthes will say of the *Text*, "theory, critical combat, and pleasure simultaneously . . . with intellectual things (*RB*, 90). As Montaigne says earlier in the essay from which I have taken the passage commented upon, "The one who does not guide others well, guides himself well; *and the one who cannot produce effects, writes Essays*" (emphasis mine). Our question—What logic permits the heterogeneous fragments of the essayistic text to constitute a unity?—should, then, be posed more specifically in these terms:

(1) What is the constitutive method of the essayistic text?
(2) What sort of effects does it intend?

On these questions, the *Essays* are quite clear:

> The ancients do not fear these changes, and with a wonderful grace
> they let themselves be tossed in the wind, *or seem to*. (III. 9, 761, em-
> phasis mine)

It is possible to interpret the reservations expressed by the words "or seem to" as a deliberate calculation on Montaigne's part—to say that Montaigne, either by natural inclination or by conviction, would find pleasure in leading his reader astray, all the while knowing perfectly well where he is going and where he is taking his reader. Such a reservation is generally credited to the account of that Montaigne who is considered to be a strategist of meaning and an apologist of digressive allusion, in order to assert some continuity of meaning between his diverse fragments. In short, this passage can be interpreted in the most economical sense: one need but read between the lines to understand that there is an underlying idea structuring the text. Such an interpretation seems to be confirmed by the third sequence of the text quoted above: "It is the inattentive reader who loses my subject, not I." The author remains master of meaning.

There are at least three arguments that weaken such an interpretation. (1) It leaves no place for the productivity linked to the intrinsic form of the essay. (2) It disregards Montaigne's affirmation of the writer's status with regard to the text: "To him," writes Montaigne of the poet-essayist, "we must certainly concede mastery and preeminence in speech" (III. 9, 761). (3) In addition, such an interpretation should be categorically rejected because its underlying assumptions—that the text is based on the author's pleasure in leading the reader astray and on his ultimate mastery of the text's meaning—inevitably lead to the evasion of the other difficulties presented by the text. Thus Montaigne, seeking to make his thought clear, writes:

> The titles of my chapters do not always embrace their matter; often
> they only denote it by *some mark*, like those other titles, *The Maid of
> Andros*, *The Eunuch*, etc. (III. 9, 761, emphasis mine)

It is possible to see here no more than a kind of casual indifference to the stylistic or rhetorical rule concerning the relation between the *title of a work* and the *content of the work* itself, an indifference that may be accounted for simply enough in aesthetic or psychological terms. Thus René Jasinski can write, commenting on this passage: "Assuredly the title does not work without a touch of imagination [*fantaisie*]. . . . But let us *modify the title*. Let us underline the humor in *Of Coaches*. Or let us *substitute* another title that corresponds to the deep meaning! . . . Everything becomes immediately clear."[9]

By asserting the "deep meaning" of the text, hypostasized *against* the multiplicity of facets and the multitude of thoughts and ideas it produces, the *form* of the text is once more denied any productivity of its own. In such an approach, there is an instrumental conception of the expository mode of a work that makes for a quick resolution of the problems.[10] Remove this, change that: but what remains of the work? Why did the essayist choose this mode of presentation and organization of his thoughts if one can so easily suppress everything that, according to the familiar stereotyped canons, is taken for pure ornamentation or a slip of the pen?

Clearly, we must follow a different path if we are to understand what is taking place in the *Essays*. Montaigne says of his titles that they "denote by *some mark*" the matter of the *Essays*. Why not take him seriously and try to discover what this "mark" may allude to and what its significance may be?

In my opinion, the answer to this question can be found in the third sequence of the text I have quoted above, where Montaigne writes: "It is the inattentive reader who loses my subject, not I."

This is an affirmation that one spontaneously tends to interpret as follows: the montage of stories, examples, and so on in the essay, the exploded and chaotic aspect of construction, are surface effects; in fact, Montaigne always knows where he is going. All that's necessary is to find *the* guiding thread. This sort of interpretation resembles those discussed earlier: again, the author's intention becomes the central "motif" of the essay and the rest is relegated to the simple role of ornamental "grotesques": stories, examples, and so on.

Only in the language of paradox can it be said that an essay is "tossed in the wind" and *at the same time* that it merely "seems" to be "tossed." Indeed, the most characteristic feature of a Montaignian essay is this altogether original kind of "disjunctive synthesis" (Deleuze) of opposite terms, contradictory fragments, and the like. But to accept and understand this, one must see the difference between the instances that Montaigne calls arbitrary — "fortuitous," as he puts it — and those he calls necessary. The essayist in Montaigne — and the "secret" of the genre he created is to be found principally at this level — does not affirm that the *same thing* is both necessary and arbitrary: *"necessity" always refers to the mode of exposition, constitution, and functioning* of the always heterogeneous elements of the essayistic text, *whereas "arbitrary"* refers only to what the text sets forth ("thoughts," "ideas," "judgments," etc.), elements that "fall" like simple effects of the work's functioning and that must be connected first of all to its formal structure.

Neither the "deep meaning" nor the psychological identity of the author, nor the "style" are of real use in showing that *in spite of everything* there is unity and meaning in the essayistic work. One must have recourse instead to the particular mode of treatment or arrangement of the stories, examples, maxims, and other elements. The structuration of the essay in no way originates in a dualist logic of content and form, latent and patent, an opposition between deep and surface structure: it cannot be said that the chaotic succession of the elements entering into the essay's composition is arbitrary only in appearance and actually becomes a necessary order for the attentive reader. There is not first an idea or concept that is then followed by "illustrations" made up of anecdotes, witticisms, quotations, and the like. Instead, *from the very beginning and at an identical semantic and formal level*, there are heterogeneous series of stories, examples, maxims, and the rest.

What Montaigne affirms as necessary, first and foremost—and this is the theoretical affirmation running through the *Essays*—is *chaos*, or, in Montaigne's own terms, "diversity": "And two opinions identical in the world never existed, any more than two hairs or two grains," writes Montaigne, concluding his first published book. *"Their most universal quality is diversity."*[11] What *returns*, what comes again—while remaining quite irreducible to a punctual identity of the psychological, gnoseological, or material type is Chaos—the multiplicity and diversity of suppositions, words, ideas, and things, the infinite variations of reality and life. To realize this, one need only interrogate "things" by going beyond the concepts that are supposed to "express" them:

> I ask what is "nature," "pleasure," "circle," "substitution." The question is one of words, and is answered in the same way. "A stone is a body." But if you pressed on: "And what is a body?"—"Substance."—"And what is substance?" and so on, you would finally drive the respondent to the end of his lexicon. (III. 13, 818–819)

The method of exposition and composition of the essay and the type of effects corresponding to it are in the image of this multiplicity, this variety, and it is this that makes their character fundamentally paradoxical for us. For instead of affirming the identity and the return of the "idea," the "thought," or the "intention" *one* and *united*, the form of the essay, inverting the classic problematic of the exposition of the *Idea* in general, is such that it can affirm the identity and the "eternal" return only of a chaos in which several ideas will shine, in which several "bold" subjects will be born, but this time in a totally "fortuitous" manner:

> Lord, what beauty there is in these lusty sallies and this variation, and more so, the more nonchalant and fortuitous they seem. (III. 9, 761)

For this reason, attention must be given to the formulation of Montaigne's poetic theses. Thus, Montaigne does not say: the *reader in general* can "lose my subject," but rather the "inattentive" reader. From what I have tried to show, the inattentive reader is not at all, quite obviously, the careless, casual, or unintelligent reader, but rather the one who expects the essayistic work to produce only effects with a monological or singular meaning. The "inattentive" reader is also the one who expects the essayist to affirm from the first the unity in origin of the essay's preexisting and self-evident contents – in short, to settle matters once and for all. Finally, the "inattentive" reader is the one who reverses the perspective by taking a given "fallout" (*retombée*), a given punctual effect that the essay produces in the course of reading, as the text's *meaning* or the author's *intention*. Thus the reader generalizes the *partial effects* that are produced by the literary machine at work in the essay and takes them as the essay's meaning.[12]

BASTANT, ANTE. adj. Sufficient. *Renaut n'en prit qu'une somme bastante* [Renaut took only a sufficient sum]. LA FONT. *Orais. Louville, avec Mme Maintenon contraire, n'était pas bastant pour être de la conférence* [Louville, with Mme Maintenon opposed, was not strong enough to prevail]. ST. SIM, 101, 75 *Obsolete*.

HIST. 16 c. *D'autres forces assez bastantes pour faire un avant-garde* [Other forces strong enough to form a vanguard]. CARL. I, 40. *Aux besoins extraordinaires, toutes les provisions du monde n'y scauraient baster* [All the provisions in the world cannot suffice for extraordinary needs]. MONT. I, 317. *Cette âme sera capable d'une très saincte amitié, la sincérité et la solidité de ses moeurs y sont déjà bastantes* [This soul will be capable of a very holy amity, the sincerity and solidity of its ways are already enough]. ID. III, 73.

ETYM. Ital. *bastare* 'to suffice, to endure, to be preserved'; from a root meaning 'to sustain, to bear', found also in *bât* 'packsaddle', *bâtir* 'to build', *bâton* 'stick, staff' q.v.

—LITTRE

BASTANT, ANTE. adj. The *s* is pronounced. That which suffices, which suits, which satisfies. *Ces vivres ne sont pas bastantes pour me nourrir* [These provisions are not enough to feed me]. *Ces raisons ne sont pas bastantes pour me persuader* [These reasons aren't sufficent to convince me]. *Cette caution n'est pas bastante pour me contenter* [This guarantee isn't enough to satisfy me].

BASTER. The *s* is pronounced. Formerly meant to 'to suffice' and is still used in the proverbial phrase *Baste pour cela* 'who cares!' or simply *Baste* 'pass, I'm satisfied.' This word came into use only in the time of Queen Catherine de Médicis, as Borel notes.

—FURETIERE, *Dictionnaire Universel*, 1690
(Slaktine Reprints, Geneva, 1970)

Although he refuses any explanation that relies on the singleness of the author, meaning, or "style," Montaigne does not revert to the mere attentiveness of the reader to account for the unity of the work. He does not surreptitiously reintroduce on the one hand what he rejects on the other. What is it, then, that makes one have the experience, in spite of everything, that the arrangement of the heterogeneous parts that constitute an essay forms a certain *totality*?

At first, Montaigne's answer to the question may appear sybilline:

Some word about it will always be found off in a corner, which will not fail to be sufficient (*bastant*), although it may be concise. (III. 9, 761)

What can be the nature of such a "word"? How can a word be said to be "sufficient"? Further, what must the power of a word be to give a text as fragmented as an essay the principle of its organization and justify its motley appearance? This is clarified in another text, where Montaigne deals with the unity so characteristic of the essayistic work:

My book is *always one*. Except that at each new edition, so that the buyer may not come off completely empty-handed, *I allow myself to add, since it is only an ill-fitted patchwork, some supernumerary emblems*. (III. 9, 736, emphasis mine)

Once more Montaigne gives us to understand in the form of a paradox the specificity of the unity of his *Essays*: the book is always one and yet it is an "ill-fitted patchwork." The "soldering" (*soudume*)—a favorite term in Montaigne—is always lacking, and yet the essay is not constituted in an arbitrary manner: somewhere, there is always a "sufficient word" (*mot bastant*), a "concise" word, a "supernumerary emblem" that enables the essay to function as a totality and gives it its unity. But the "sufficient word" is not the latent or original meaning that one can always end up finding again with a little "attentiveness"; it is a "paradoxical element" of the "Snark" or "Jabberwocky" type: it is a complicated word—that is, a word that *complicates* stories, *envelops* significations, conceals riches that no preconceived notion will ever subsume. The "sufficient" word is a Pandora's box from which anything and everything may escape, but whose contents can never be known in advance. For this reason, its potentialities can be deployed only by means of certain *literary strategies*, certain ways in which stories and thoughts are brought together in a montage.

To situate in a theoretical context what we understand by the expressions "sufficient word" or "supernumerary emblem," we may turn to the concept elaborated by Gilles Deleuze, under the categories of the *dark precursor* or *Differentiator*, in his *Différence et Répétition*.[13] "Every system," Deleuze writes, "contains its dark precursor that assures communication between border series. . . . In every case it is a matter of knowing how the precursor exercises this role" (156–157). A little further on, Deleuze adds: "We call *disparate* [*dispars*] the dark precursor, this *difference in itself* (to the second degree) that brings into relation the series that are themselves heterogeneous or disparate. In each instance, its space of displacement and its process of disguise are what determine the relative magnitude of the differences brought into relation."

Now, a careful reading of Montaigne's texts will show that there is nothing less arbitrary than the choice of *titles* or "words" that Montaigne assembles in order to submit them to multiple variations. Contrary to Jasinski, who sees arbitrariness in Montaigne's choice of titles, I would be inclined to say that nothing is more essential to the play of the text (in other instances this can be a word or notion constantly running through the text: "experience," "coach," etc.) than the choice of a given title—but with the essential reservation that such a "title" no longer acts through its *identity*, whether the identity be "nominal" or "homonymic." Indeed, as frequently occurs in Montaigne, the title no longer appears as the identity of a signified, of an "obviated" theme, but, according to Deleuze's rigorous formulation, as the "differentiator" of distinct signifieds, which "*secondarily* produce an effect of resemblance of the signifieds as an effect of identity in the signifier" (ibid.)—and, I might add, in the word, notion, or title. In Montaigne—at least as I read him with reference to Deleuze—the "differentiator" in question may equally well be called "sufficient word," "concise word," or "supernumerary emblem" because these words and "emblems" play identical roles in the economy of a Montaignian text.

Take as an example the essay entitled "Of Drunkenness"(II. 2)—the majority of Montaigne's essays could be similarly analyzed. Between the *signifying* series of "vices" and the *signified* series of different types of "intoxication" that Montaigne, seemingly improvising, parades before us, no equality, no semantic identity is established: of the two series paired by the dark precursor "drunkenness," one always exceeds or stimulates the indeterminate character of the other. Better: the respective determinations of each series are constantly exchanged with those of the others without ever reaching equilibrium. To put it another way: no prior definition of "vice" can ever exhaust the indefinite "variety" of figures (and effects) of intoxication. Without the potency of the esoteric word "intoxication," the essay—the text of this essay—would have been impossible. But this is because the text is literally nourished by the gap (*écart*)—or, if you prefer, the (irreducible, generative) difference—that the word "drunkenness" establishes by assembling a multitude of themes that without it could never have been brought together. Faced with the infinite variety of figures assumed by "intoxication," where can we *pigeonhole*, how above all can we *qualify* the given forms it may take: intoxication that is *poetic*, or *prophetic*, and so on? Clearly, it is not enough to assert that the essay is a mode of incompletion or simply that it is "informal": this is the same illusion that leads us to say that a text does not belong to any *genre* and to accept the existing genres as necessary forms. It is not by its rhetorical deficiency, but rather by the excess of forms it brings into play, that the essay invents the *form* in which, as I shall seek to demonstrate, it plays in its turn the role of "precursor"—that is to say, in which, by mobilizing the resources of multiple genres at the same time, it provokes, as Barthes puts it, a veritable "mutation" of the modern text. Here is the first part of the answer to the question of the essay's unity:

the "sufficient" word can in no way be dissociated from the series (of stories, examples, maxims, dialogues, poems, and the rest) that it puts into play. The very logic of the paradoxical and "sufficient" word is to render obsolete and insignificant the rhetorical question of the beginning and the end, the before and the after, as prerequisite to any possible narration or discourse. Moreover, in this logic of the "sufficient" word, the rhetorical frontier separating the proper meaning from the figural, the metaphorical from the literal, and above all, the narrative from the discursive, no longer exists. In an essay, one can think and "discourse" with stories, poems, metaphors, and myths. The "sufficient" word always plays on at least two series of heterogeneous significations, making them resonate and communicate without, however, being their cause; it complicates things by multiplying stories, and within them, it brings about new distinctions by having each series branch into new series of other stories.

Now it can be seen why the logic of the essay is a logic of *complicatio*: through a paradoxical word heterogeneous series are put into communication and made to resonate without being subsumed. But there will always be a hiatus between the series, and only the "sufficient" word will maintain a connection between them. The starting point is this genre of "words"—"drunkenness," "cripple," and the rest—though the essayist is interested not in their meaning but in the "worlds" they enclose. Thus the essay takes on a given scope, follows a given path, etc., proportional to the subjects that are "complicated" in this way. Its entire "organization"—as well as its effects—depends on this. Thus it is a false problem to look for the plan of an essay. Finding a coherent one—which is not at all impossible—can happen only by chance.

There is one pitfall to be avoided: it is possible to give the "sufficient word" an identity and simplicity that distort comprehension of the overall mechanism at work in the essay. With the "sufficient word," contrary to what happens for a concept, stories remain complicated at the same time that series continue to be separated. And regardless of the operations effected on the basis of a paradoxical word, it does not cease to complicate those series it brings into relation, despite their heterogeneity, and to multiply their significations. The flash of light is always apparent, but not the "dark precursor" that announces it.[14] More specifically: this type of "dark precursor," the "sufficient word," is sought after in order to complicate things, and not to simplify them or lessen their import. The aim is not to make the reader's task easier, but rather to teach how to decipher the signification of words that spring out of chaos and the "perpetual movement" of all things. It is for this reason that the essay is drawn to images and metaphors. For this reason, it can only manifest itself—in every sense of the term—through fragments:

> I do not want a man to use his strength making me attentive and to shout at me fifty times: "*Or oyez!*" ["Now listen"] in the manner of our

heralds. The Romans used to say in their religion *"Hoc age"* ["Give Heed"], as we say in ours *"Sursum corda"* ["Lift up your hearts"]: these are so many words lost on me. (II. 10, 301)

The essayist wants "to deal with people who themselves have told themselves this (to 'give heed'); or who, if they have their *'Hoc age,'* have a substantial one with a body of its own" (ibid., 302). The "simple and artless" style that Montaigne defends will be that which "strikes": "difficult rather than boring, remote from affectation, irregular, disconnected, and bold; each bit making a body in itself; not pedantic, not monkish, not lawyer-like, but rather soldierly" (I. 26, 127). The problem of the compositional originality of an essay is not resolved by changing the title, by drastically carving up the text, or by having recourse to psychologemes! Suppressing or simply changing the title of an essay such as "Of Coaches" only discards a bothersome word: what makes up the unity of the text is broken; it is reduced to formless *patchwork*.

2. From the "Sufficient Word" to the "Mana-Word"

A term may be formulated only one time in the entire work, but
nevertheless through the effect of a certain number of transformations
that define the structural fact, be there "everywhere" and "always."
(Roland Barthes, *Critique et vérité*, 67)

When Barthes wants to designate the organizing principle of the logic at work in the essay, he always summons the same word: the word "body." But, as in Montaigne, this is never to designate an inscribed totalization or a synthesis of other words. What Deleuze says about the "esoteric word" may be said of the "body" in Barthes: it is never where it is sought, and conversely, it is never found where it is. *It is lacking in its place* (Lacan). But "it is lacking (also) in its own identity, it is lacking in its own similarity, it is lacking in its own origin."[15] But let us first read what Barthes himself tells us about it:

In an author's lexicon, will there not be a word-as-mana, a word whose ardent, complex, ineffable, and somehow sacred signification gives the illusion that by this one word one might answer for everything? Such a word is neither eccentric nor central; it is motionless and carried, floating, never *pigeonholed*, always atopic . . . at once remainder and supplement, a signifier taking up the place of every signified. . . . This word-as-mana is the word "body" (*RB*, 129–130).

It is these qualities and exceptional powers that designate the body as the organ of gap and difference, the organ of "irreducible difference," as Barthes says in the same text, and also, consequently, "the principle of all structuration (since structuration is what is Unique in structure)" (*RB*, 175). Clarifying this major point, Barthes goes on to say:

> If I managed to talk politics *with my own body*, I should make out of the most banal of (discursive) structures a structuration; with repetition, I should produce Text. (ibid.)

In this way, the Barthesian essay organizes the different sorts of "words" entering into its composition around a quite specific word. But what is interesting in this "repetition" of a movement already noted in Montaigne is that, this time, operating in a completely different historical and theoretical context, it enables us to bring to the fore the incircumscribable character of this "word" and to understand how the structuration of the essayistic text is brought about on the basis of an atopic instance.

If each difference and each gap – and consequently the proliferation of signs in the essay – originate in the body as mana-word, it is first of all because we have several bodies (*PT*, 16). Far from being reduced to the ectodermic frontiers or plates of the anatomists or physiologists, the body is also a body of bliss [*jouissance*]. Thus, originally, is difference hollowed out: a different discourse corresponds to each body. A primary series of gaps therefore resides in the body as exoteric object: no movement, no word can suture the gap separating the loving or erotic body, for example, from the body of needs. Therefore, as a result of the irreducibility of desire to need, the body appears as a "plural" instance (*RB*, 60).

But another series duplicates this first series of differences by overdetermining its fundamental features: irreducible to a sum of functions or organs, the body is no longer reducible to a pure exteriority: as erotic body, it has the form of a *text*. It is already a figure wherein any temptation to go back to a simple origin is engulfed. In this way, it can be said that the text has "human form"; it is "a figure, an anagram of the body" (*PT*, 17). But the converse is also true: the body can be considered as a "figure":

> As supplement, the body is the site of the transgression effected by the narrative: it is at the level of the body that the two *inconciliabilia* of the Antithesis (outside and inside, cold and heat, death and life) are brought together, are made to touch, to mingle in the most amazing of figures. (*S/Z*, 28)

This mingling at the origin of body/text – the text as a "certain body" – determines others: for example, the mingling of *body* (*corps*) and *corpus*: "The *corpus*: what a splendid idea! Provided one was willing to read *the body* in the corpus" (*RB*, 161); or the mingling of *body* and *citation*: "Every body is a citation: of the "already-written." The origin of desire is the statue, the painting, the image" (*S/Z*, 33).

There are other interminglings of the same sort in Barthes's work, and we shall certainly encounter them. But what we may note now is that each renews the same paradigmatic opposition: BODY/TEXT(S) or BODY/LANGUAGE(S). This clearly means that the body is no longer opposed to the soul, to the *psyché*, or to any other spiritual instance—in short, as the material and external opposed to the psychological and internal. But this also means—and it is significant—that as it is for Montaigne and above all for Nietzsche,[16] the body is neither a simple origin nor a substance, but the site of atopia: the site where one can change "postures" and "perspectives" endlessly without any of them being obliged to submit to a hierarchy or unified subject. In general, as Barthes says, there is no *Ursuppe*: there is neither an original soup nor an original text. The "original" language is already a plurality of texts that mutually communicate, anastomose, or quote each other. For Barthes, this is Gide, and also Nietzsche, Balzac, Proust, and Michelet: the list is necessarily open. How do I know which text—or which *body*—I do not want? Nothing can determine in advance in which body or in which text it is found. It is always after the event (*après-coup*), through writing, through reading that we find out. For want of doing this work—alone, for here no one can "stand in" for us (Proust)—we sacrifice our "language life": "His place (his *milieu*) is language: that is where he accepts or rejects, that is where his body *can* or *cannot*" (*RB*, 53).

If we are obliged to read the (word) "body" (*corps*) in the word "corpus," no more limits can be assigned to the investigation of what determines us as text, as body, or as subject: for in an absolutely original sense, the "norm" is henceforth quite "formal" or *textual*: it resides in the spacing out, the different degrees of the text—its "layering," as Barthes says. In mobilizing an infinite corpus, the discourse of the essay is a generalized exploration of the body by means of the most diverse languages. Inversely, the reading of an essay is the experimentation of a different body, of a different imaginary:

> At least some examples? One envisions a vast, collective harvest: bring together all the texts *which have given pleasure to someone* (wherever these texts come from) and display this textual body (*corpus*: the right word), in something like the way in which psychoanalysis has exhibited man's erotic body. (*PT*, 34)

As relay for the hordes of words of every sort that the essay mobilizes—color-words, transitional words, fashion words, value-words, etc.—we always find the body as the mana-word that no meaning can exhaust. In Montaigne, 'Nature' is the same type of word; in Nietzsche, it is Dionysus or the Will to Power. In neither instance is it ever *given*; it must be produced counter to the other words: truth (of the story), validity (of systems and structures), in a word counter to the system of representations that mask it, occult it literally and in every sense, that is to say, principally as TEXT(S).[17] Many other texts of Barthes's "narrate" in the tone of the novelistic or intimate journal the slow structuration of the essayistic text from the mana-word: "the cuttlefish and its ink."

> Sometimes he feels like letting all this language rest—this language which is in his head, in his work, in other people, as if language itself were an exhausted limb of the human body; it seems to him that if he could take a rest from language, he could rest altogether, dismissing all crises, echoes, exaltations, injuries, reasonings, etc. (*RB*, 177)

> And yet (a frequent trick of any social accusation), what is an idea for him, if not a *flush of pleasure*? Abstraction is in no way contrary to sensuality. (*RB*, 103)

> When I have a headache, perhaps it means that I am a victim of a partial desire, as if I were fetishizing a specific point of my body: *the inside of my head*: does it mean, then, that I am in an unhappy/amorous relation with my work? (*RB*, 124–125)

> My body itself (and not only my ideas) can *make up to* words, can be in some sense created by them: today, I discover on my tongue a red patch which appears to be an abrasion, or in medical terms an excoriation—painless, moreover, which fits in perfectly, I decide, with cancer! But examined closely, this sign is merely a faint desquamation of the whitish film which covers the tongue. I cannot swear that this whole little obsessive scenario has not been worked up in order to use that rare word, so attractive by dint of its exactitude: *excoriation*. (*RB*, 152)

So, we have been forewarned: at every moment we risk being "taken" by the play of the text and lost in its tiniest fold. As Corpus, the text slowly becomes an invitation to the playful exchange of our "physiology" for another, our phantasmatic for another. Therefore it is not absurd here to give, like so many lexicalized "physiologemes" or verbalized physical postures, the succession of these fragments (of texts). Such is the "migraine"—the state/the word—which is not only an extrinsic somatic sickness, but a manner of entering "just a little way," as Barthes says, into a mortal sickness for man: "Insolvency of symbolization" (*RB*, 125).

Thus, reflecting upon the substratum and the shifting foundations of his pathos and his affects, the essayist always discovers a plurality of signs and a multiplicity of words. Conversely, the fact that language may be assimilated in discourse to "an exhausted limb of the human body" or that an idea can be "thought" only by being felt beforehand as a "flush of pleasure" indicates clearly the nature of the signs that come into play in an essay: regardless of their nature they all must express a body-state and function as *biographemes*: "nothing but a factitious anamnesis: the one I lend to the author I love" (*RB*, 109). And, let us add, also the one I attribute to the reader I love and for whom I write: "By much the same sense, he imagines each time he writes something that *he will hurt one of his friends—never the same one, it changes*" (*RB*, 48–49, emphasis mine.)

But it can already be seen that this author and this reader no longer owe anything at all to the authors and readers offered us by the history of literature: the essayistic text, product of a "lexeography," is defined as *pleasure* and not as the genesis of a meaning, and its writing will find its starting point in that which "hangs together well" (*SFL*, 7) in the texts read. The turns of phrase running through it and the words constituting it no longer refer to the author as origin or to the reader as destination, but to the mana-word inasmuch as it complicates a "plural of 'charms' " or as "the site of a few tenuous details, the source of vivid novelistic glimmerings, a discontinuous chart of amiabilities" (*SFL*, 8).

In this sense, *the form of the Barthesian essay* can be *neither monumental nor finished*: for this, the subject of the enunciation would have to be originally identical to itself and a "last word" would have to be proffered. But as we know, taking the Body as "model" and "origin" (the Body as an unsaturable esoteric word and as an inexhaustible exoteric thing), the essayist writes from pure difference. The origin is gap, or, if you prefer, "différance": that is to say, text always and into infinity. In addition, a unique and unified addressee would be necessary. But as we shall see shortly, the essayist addresses *all possible* readers and not a specific one or a particular group, by organizing elements stemming from a plural word that permits the collection and arrangement of all types of possible discourses.

3. Gestures of the Idea: The Logic of Intellectual Objects

What is the nature of the "elements" that enter into an essay's composition? A series of *exempla* borrowed from Barthes gives us a glimpse:

> It is a good thing, he thought, that out of consideration for the reader, there should pass through the essay's discourse, from time to time, a sensual object (as in *Werther*, where suddenly there appear a dish of green peas cooked in butter and a peeled orange separated into sections). A double advantage: sumptuous appearance of a materiality and a distortion, a sudden gap wedged into the intellectual murmur. (*RB*, 135)

As seen in this text—and in the texts to be considered shortly—the "objects" used by the essayist are not drawn from a particular genre or domain: they can be taken from any semantic or cultural register: history, literature, painting, philosophy, sports, film, cooking—whatever you like. And, consequently, they are distinguished only by the way they are inserted into the essay's discourse. But, generally, they are constituted as specific objects by the *gap* they manifest in relation to a semantic or rhetorical norm: an unexpected or incongruous parallel between semes or heterogeneous lexemes—brain of a child/milky blossom of a camellia; subreption of a semantically overdetermined word in a context heterogeneous to it, an object glued on a painted canvas; a sketch in a graphematic succession,[18] use of a foreign phrase in everyday discourse;[19] a dialogue in a theoretical or action discourse and, generally, a passage from one genre to another or a telescoping together of two heterogeneous genres,[20] the intervention and invention of neologisms from Latin or Greek roots: stereography, logography, arthrology, semioclasty, bathmology, etc.; the use of rare or technical words in a biographical piece: anamnesis, the imaginary, excoriation, etc.

It seems that the specificity of the essay's "objects" must not be sought in the way they are produced and engendered (*Inventio*), but rather in their arrangement (*Dispositio*). And in this sense the essay falls essentially into the same category as works of collage—montage of heterotopic elements.[21] But in fact matters are not so simple, for by not taking his "objects" from an inventory of *performed* messages but from a potential inventory and thus always dealing with *codes* in the strict sense or with "strong" systems, the essayist keeps the poetician from exhibiting the discursive objects that he manipulates *independently* of the "system" from which they are taken: for example, from presenting the "theory" of "elements" on the one hand and their arrangement on the other. If such were the case the essayist "would be no more than the author of a system (what is called a philosopher, a savant, or a thinker)": and the essay a "setting up of a ritual, i.e., a rhetoric" (*SFL*, 5). But nothing of the sort: if there is a logic characteristic of the Barthesian essay, it no longer refers to a (philosophical) system; if there are "elements," they are homogeneous to neither concept nor Idea. Everything occurs as if at every moment a "fundamental structure of gap"[22] were questioning the double temptation offered by classical "system" and classical rhetoric: the closure of the text as Totality and the mastery of meaning as Truth. To put it another way, even if the "sensual objects" are recognizable in themselves and do not present any intrinsic semantic particularity, the logic of their arrangement is itself original. Therefore, the contradictory nature of these elements must be analyzed in greater detail.

> Different from the "concept" and from the "notion," which are purely ideal, the *intellectual object* is created by a kind of leverage upon the signifier: once I *take seriously* such forms as an etymology, a derivation, a metaphor, I can create a kind of *word-thought* for myself which will ferret through all my language. This word-object is both *vested* (desired) and *superficial* (employed, not explored); it has a ritual existence; as if, at a certain moment, I had *baptized* it with my sign. (*RB*, 134–135)

Conversion of Value into Theory (distractedly, I read on my file card: "convulsion," which is fine too): one might say, parodying Chomsky, that all Value is *rewritten* (⟶) as Theory. This conversion—this convulsion—is an energy (an *energon*): discourse is produced by this translation, this imaginary displacement, this creation of an alibi. (*RB*, 179)

Gestures of the idea: The Lacanian subject (for instance) never makes him think of Tokyo; but Tokyo makes him think of the Lacanian subject. . . . Philosophy then is no more than a reservoir of particular images, of ideal fictions (he borrows objects, not reasonings). Mallarmé speaks of "gestures of the idea": he finds the gesture first (expression of the body), then the idea (expression of the culture, of the intertext). (*RB*, 99)

Here then are at least three texts (there are others) where the question of the essay's "objects" (intellectual? sensuous?) is approached head-on. At first glance the proposed definition raises as many problems as it solves. What are the rules, for example, governing this convulsive "re-writing" of Value into Theory? In what way can it be said that what is "originated" in Value is as *founded* as in Theory? What kind of "value" is in question? But also: What is this "abstraction" that relays the sensuous object? What is the nature of this "gesture" as *expression* of the body? Do they indicate a simple return to a theory of the text as expression (of thought, of body)? Do they initiate an ontology of the body? Finally, do they refer to a prelinguistic or prediscursive "world"?

All of these questions are inextricably linked: on them depends the clarification of the nature of the "objects" populating the essay and the "logic" linking them: indeed, in one essay (*RB*, 72) "preciously ambiguous" semes are taken up again, rewritten from one fragment to the next. But contrary to what would occur for the concepts of a philosophical system, for example, the semes are never taken up in order to define or exhaust them. In each instance, they play a new role, carrying along other signifieds, summoning other codes. In each case, everything is there, "but floating."[23] As the words—amphibologies, antitheses, the Arabic *addâd* ("words each of which has two absolutely contrary meanings" [*RB*, 73]), enantiosemes, etc.—are selected and scrutinized, the discourse *is produced* as a "translation" of these words in an "other site" and as an unfolding of all their potentialities. At an initial stage, the only rule is that of entropy: "to keep a meaning from 'taking' " (*RB*, 148). In the interval—between two fragments, between two words, two objects—it is the *body* that "reconciles the *inconciliabilia*," but never to the advantage of a third term of synthesis or of a concept. Indeed, what allows the body to be thought of as a third atopic term is the passage from a dialectic with two terms to "another dialectic" whose ruling principle is this: "everything comes back, but it comes back as Fiction" (*RB*, 69). This dialectic is elsewhere called "subtle subversion" and is characterized as follows:

By *subtle subversion* I mean . . . what is not directly concerned with destruction, evades the paradigm, and seeks some *other* term: a third term, which is not, however, a synthesizing term but an eccentric extraordinary term. (*PT*, 55)

We know that for Barthes there is a means other than the invention of this type of third "deporting" term (*terme de déport*) for going beyond the "exasperated" binarism from which meaning generally proceeds: marked/unmarked, white/black, homosexual/heterosexual, and the like. We can escape the "paradigm" and mechanistic dualism through "supplementation" (Balzac with Zambinella), through an "escape towards the real" (the Racinian confidant abolishing the tragic antithesis) and also through the intervention of the *category of Neutral*.[24] Regardless of the means, the logic is the same: disturbing the "good conscience of language," questioning the important objects of Knowledge (Nature, History, Truth), and subverting the set of classic canonical oppositions. What ultimately determines the constitution of the essay's "objects" as "gestures of the idea" and enables us to understand that what distinguishes them from the theoretical concept or the philosophical category is a new "logic," a new type of *arrangement* of "words" (Mikhaïl Bakhtin) that come into play in the constitution of the essayistic text.

What is an *intellectual* object? What is a *sensual* object? A creation of "alibis," of "other sites (rhetorical, physical)" (*RB*, 73); that is to say, *the translation into value* of a word (of an object) that is either *overdetermined*, theoretically or ideologically—and this is what Barthes calls an *intellectual* object—or *underdetermined* and even undetermined—and then we are dealing with a *sensuous* object. The essential point is that, before designating or expressing a meaning, both kinds of object *incarnate* an "intensity" or, more precisely, a *difference of intensity* between two impressions or between two fundamentally heterogeneous registers: "plus" or "minus."

Another question remains to be clarified: how do these words, these objects become *values*? What is the instance allowing one to say they have their origin in value? Barthes is unambiguous on this point:

How does the word become value? *At the level of the body.* The theory of this carnal word was given in his *Michelet*: this historian's vocabulary, the array of his value-words, is organized by a *physical thrill*, the *taste or distaste* for certain historical *bodies*. Thus he creates, by the interposition of a variable complication, certain "favorite" *words*, "favorable" words (in the magical sense of the adjective), "marvelous" words (brilliant and felicitous). Like transitional objects, they are of *uncertain status*; actually it is a kind of *absence of the object, of meaning, that they stage*: despite the hardness of their contours, the strength of their repetition, they are *vague, floating words*; they are trying to become fetishes. (*RB*, 130, emphasis mine).

The rule of "rewriting value into theory" thus has nothing mysterious about it: it consists principally in putting into play the logic that I attempted to bring to the fore earlier: that of the body as mana-word producing an indefinite series of other words, without ever making a Totality out of them and without receiving an ultimate meaning from them in return. For, no longer owing anything to the concept or the theoretical notion as such, intellectual and sensual objects no longer have as their function predicating the mana-word or fulfilling its form. On the contrary, these paradoxical objects become possible and are capable of being predicated only thanks to this word *that complicates them all*: it is also thanks to this atopic instance that they occupy a certain "site" (*lieu*), incarnate a certain "posture," and assume a name: *Tokyo* (—→) *Lacanian subject*.

In other words, if what is "founded in value" is so *to the same extent* as what is founded "in Theory," this is essentially due to the fact that sensual or intellectual objects obey a logic and an expository method that no longer owe anything to the economy of philosophical "system":[25] they find their justification and the principle of their efficacy in the rewriting mechanism that reproduces them by reinscribing them "elsewhere": beyond "oppressive meaning" and "paraded meaning" (*RB*, 124) and generally "outside all codes because they continually invent their own" (*PT*, 15).

I can now name the "abstraction" that relays the "sensual object": it is the "intellectual object" — generally a concept borrowed from the (theoretical, psychoanalytic, philosophical) culture of the moment — inasmuch as it over-codes and re-marks every "object" that it "takes aslant" and "the effect of overdetermination" (*RB*, 85) it authorizes. By associating Tokyo with the Lacanian Subject, the essayist makes an "allocutionary connection" (Hubert Damisch) between two heterogeneous registers that no "scientific" or purely "theoretical" discourse can permit. Are some examples needed?

Coming from psychoanalysis and seeming to remain there, "*transference*," nonetheless, readily leaves the Oedipal situation. The Lacanian "*image-repertory*" — *imaginaire* — extends to the borders of the classical "self-love" — *amour-propre*. "*Bad faith*" leaves the Sartrian system. . . . "*Bourgeois*" receives the whole Marxist accent, but keeps overflowing toward the aesthetic and the ethical. (*RB*, 74)

Thus, far from implying a return to a theory of *expression* that originates in a self-conscious "body" or a self that is self-identical — which derives more or less from an *ontology of the subject*, well on this side of the words and utterances that it complicates and behind any realization or completion that it seeks — the body as mana-word refers rather to an *originary scenario* in the sense that it precedes all scenes, even primordial ones, and always refers without limitation to other words and texts. Thus, the body designates above all "this inscription of difference as the opening of signs in the subject where every conceivable gap originates."[26] The body is neither the first nor the last word, but the word that couples differences, arranges gaps, and enables the production of "infinite essays":

> In this way, no doubt, words are shifted, systems communicate, moder- nity is tried [*essayée*] (the way one tries all the push buttons on a radio one doesn't know how to work), but the intertext thereby created is literally *superficial*: one adheres *liberally*. (*RB*, 74)

The veritable "taxonomic rage" animating every essayist, the extraordinary prosperity the essayist has for exhausting the lexicon, inventing neologisms, perusing encyclopedias, "pillaging" etymologies, comes from a constant anxiety "to say everything," to name everything: but "to say everything" implies here less the will to exhaust a repertory, to cram the lacunae full – which in fact would be pure "eclectism" – than to explore the full range of a "spectrum," all the phases of a circuit: that of the sites where one speaks, that of the sites where it speaks and where it writes, and finally that of the sites where it reads.

Thus, in the same movement Philosophy is rejected as a system of reasoning and is transformed into a "reservoir of images": the entire history of "human thought" – here understood as "transposition" of the history of the body into images[27] and concepts – is inscribed therein. Taken aslant, certain of its notions will be allowed to enrich a given circuit of words with their ideological and semantic charge, to supplement a given circle of fragments, a given sensual object with their theoretical "value." But this does not hold solely for the philosophical system: any system, any code or register of knowledge, *if it resonates at a given moment with a sensual object* – as gesture of the idea – can be subjected to the same treatment. "Disconnected, mimed, mocked" (*PT*, 31), all languages can work toward producing the "ideal" text that is the essay: the main thing is to keep from being trapped by the system, to keep the ability to drift, to slip from word to word, from object to object. The logic of selection and arrangement here is of a different order. The principle of efflorescence and pluralization of the text's elements rests in extraordinary words, in unnamable objects. Numerous texts in *Roland Barthes by Roland Barthes* suggest this by pointing out that as "word- thought" or "word-object," the intellectual object can be both *invested* (desired) and *superficial* – that is to say that it can be used *tactically* but never explored.

> In relation to the systems which surround him, what is he? Say an echo chamber: he reproduces the thoughts badly, he follows the words; he pays his visits, i.e., his respects, to vocabularies, he *invokes* notions, he rehearses them under a name; he makes use of this name as of an em- blem (thereby practicing a kind of philosophical ideography) and this

emblem dispenses him from following to its conclusion the system of which it is the signifier (which simply makes him a sign). (*RB*, 74)

In him, the desire for the word prevails, but this pleasure is partly constituted by a kind of doctrinal vibration. (ibid.)

The word transports me because of the notion that *I am going to do something with it*: it is the thrill of a future praxis, something like an *appetite*. This desire makes the entire motionless chart of language vibrate. (*RB*, 129)

He is not very good at getting to the heart of things. A word, a figure of thought, a metaphor, in short, a form fastens upon him for several years, he repeats it, uses it everywhere (for instance, "body," "difference," "Orpheus," "Argo," etc.) but he makes no effort to reflect further as to what he means by such words or such figures . . . you cannot get to the heart of a refrain; you can only substitute another one for it. (*RB*, 127)

One cannot read these fragments without thinking about the way Montaigne's "sufficient" word functions: a word that strictly speaking *explicates* nothing—unless this verb is taken in the sense of "ex-plicating," of unfolding—but that *complicates* because it is desired and because it is desire for the maddest images and the strongest impressions. It is in this sense that the "sufficient" word is at the heart of the "paragrammatized order"[28] that is sought for and set to work in every essay: essayistic *writing* consists more in "mobilizing an image and its opposite" (*SFL*, 111), in making use of words and following them in a continuous movement of pleasure(s), than in ploddingly reproducing the "thoughts" they are supposed to convey:

And this is what constitutes the writing of essays (we speak here of Bataille): the amorous rhythm of science and of value: heterology, bliss. (*RB*, 159)

In every case it is first of all a question of using a word as "emblem" but in the sense in which the emblem is "the insignia of an impossible recognition; that which establishes the bearer as out of place."[29] Desire, doctrinal vibration, rhythm or resonance, the word, the emblem—the word as emblem—can therefore never be assumed "for good" or "once and for all." As Robbe-Grillet says, "the Barthesian fragment shifts (*glisse*) continuously and its meaning is situated not in the bits of content that will appear here and there, but, on the contrary, *in the shifting (glissement) itself*."[30]

Here, too, it is difficult to think that the similarity in tone between Montaigne's work and Barthes's is purely fortuitous: "I do not paint being," Montaigne said,

"*I paint the passage*." But rehabilitating the essay as a genre wholly on its own and, what is more, *recapturing its form* are the achievements of Barthes alone. Born *practically* and *aesthetically* with Montaigne in France and sporadically reappearing here and there, the essay was to be "born theoretically" with Barthes; and for the first time it makes its *theoretical entrance* in the history of literature as a "reflective" text – namely, a text that "destroys utterly, *to the point of contradiction*, its own discursive category, its sociolinguistic reference (its 'genre')" (*PT*, 30). It is thus not surprising that the practice – of writing or reading, it doesn't matter which – of such a text should go hand in hand with a "new" approach to the very substance of language: "It is a matter of effecting, by transmutation (and no longer only by transformation), a new philosophic state of the language-substance; this extraordinary state, this incandescent metal, outside origin and outside communication, then becomes language, and not *a* language, whether disconnected, mimed, mocked" (*PT*, 31). In returning to the fragment, Barthes teaches us to read and understand the "hidden art" of essayistic writing.

4. The Three Entrances

The foremost constraint is to consider that *in the work everything is signifying*: a grammar is not well formulated if all the sentences cannot be explained; a system of meaning is incomplete if *all* the words cannot be assigned an intelligible place: *if one single feature is left over, it is not a good description.* (Roland Barthes, *Critique et vérité*, 65–66)

Although traversed by an infinity of complicated "words" and "objects," the Essay as a reflective text is literally occupied on the symbolic plane by only one object (that I have taken a certain liberty in naming, a certain pleasure in describing and in watching proliferate semantically): this "object" is the (word) body – the body as a plural reality irreducible to a simple entity, the body as an unsaturable manaword. The Barthesian Essay makes of the body a literary topography (surveying its different amorous "postures," its postures of reading or writing) and a complicated story. In this sense, paraphrasing Nietzsche, we could say that the Barthesian Essay deals with perhaps nothing other than the body: it is the history of literature and thought becoming sensitive to and conscious of the birth of a "superior body."[31] Conversely, we can also define the Essay "as the thinking of the body in a state of language" (*RB*, 145). First "entrance."

As "irreducible difference" and "principle of all structuration," the body itself refers to an infinity of other "objects": an indefinite number of culturally or theoretically overdetermined intellectual objects; an infinite number of indeterminate or underdetermined sensual objects whose specificity I tried to bring to the fore in relation to traditional notions: concept, idea. Second "entrance."

The merit of these two "entrances" is in designating the irreducible "elements" of the Essay and certain of their formal qualities. They enable us to define to some extent the two edges of the Essay as Text: at the "origin" a pure difference; at the "periphery" an infinity of intellectual and sensual objects that constantly exchange and complicate their values, causing them to resonate from one edge to the other.

However, a third "entrance" is possible: the one giving access to a multiplicity of figures of production and "text operators" that allow for the different "elements" I emphasized to be generated and articulated in the Barthesian essay. These operators allow us to define the minimal conditions of a *structure* in the Essay:

> How does it go, when I write? — Doubtless by movements of language sufficiently formal and repeated for me to be able to call them "figures": I divine that there are *figures of production*, text operators. Among others, these are:
> — evaluation
> — nomination
> — amphibology
> — etymology
> — paradox
> — emphasis
> — enumeration
> — tourniquet
> And here is another of such figures: *forgery* (in the jargon of graphologists, forgery is an imitation of handwriting). (*RB*, 91–92)

Whether this "enumeration" of "figures" is exhaustive is a false problem: the Essay is neither a philosophical system nor a constituted Rhetoric. It is more important to find out why these figures are, in a privileged way, considered text *operators*. In other words, it is mainly a matter of determining their function (in what type of textual organization) and their object (operating on what?).

Except for *Forgery*, which has a completely special status in the Essay, these figures are original in the sense that all have the same formal characteristics. All presuppose a "word," "object," or "reality" that is always constituted by at least two heterogeneous "edges" which the figures cause to cut or re-cut each other, assemble or separate from each other, pair with each other or diverge, etc.

This is obvious for *etymology*, for instance, which Barthes praises less for the "origin" that it is supposed to exhibit than for the *effect of superimposition* that it authorizes (*RB*, 85); this is also true for *paradox*, which, in its very etymology, displays a penchant for oppositions and conflictual realities (*RB*, 71); for *enumeration* (*RB*, 72); for *evaluation*, which either opposes or pairs writerly and readerly (*S/Z*, 4) in the same text; for *nomination*, always threatened by *regressus in infinitum*, nomination that opposes the object to its absence or names to other names (*RB*, 56). Generally, when Barthes or Montaigne take hold of a word, it is never to give it a definite or complete meaning, but always to *cut it* with others, just as insipid wine is cut with a heady variety. Whenever they encounter a word with a double entrance (enantioseme) or an opposition (paradigm), it is to draw out of it a complicated story or meaning that calls forth a multiplicity of other meanings. For example, amphibology:

> Each time he encounters *one of these double words*, R.B., on the contrary, insists on keeping both meanings, as if one were winking at the other and as if the word's meaning were in that wink, so that *one and the same word*, in *one and the same sentence*, means *at one and the same time* two different things, and so that one delights, semantically, in the one by the other. (*RB*, 72)

There follows in the same text a long enumeration of amphibologies that unfold like schemata to be filled in, programs to be implemented. Thus, as Barthes remarks on several occasions, contrary to what one might expect, "it is not polysemy which is praised and sought out; it is quite precisely amphibology, duplicity" (*RB*, 73). Thus it is clear which principle is obeyed in the selection of the various figures that serve as operators in the essayistic text: all figures will have to aid in multiplying perspectives and perpetuating the semantic duplicity that is sought. Therefore, they are all subordinated to a single one, the *figure of duplication*: double register, double thought, double band.

But, on the other hand, cross-checks, cuts or breaks, couplings or telescopings of languages and texts always take their point of departure from these two edges. These enable, through a slipping or drifting from one edge to the other of the same word, the production of extraordinary words; from one code to another, a new text. But now it must be noted that these two aspects enter into play at another level of the spiral as a *criterion of evaluation* of the Text of Modernity and of the type of pleasure derived from it:

> Sade: the pleasure of reading him clearly proceeds from certain breaks (or certain collisions): antipathetic codes (the noble and the trivial, for example) come into contact; pompous and ridiculous neologisms are created; pornographic messages are embodied in sentences so pure they might be used as grammatical models. As textual theory has it: the language is redistributed. (*PT*, 6)

When the time comes, we will have to account for the "clarity" that is referred to and specify the nature of these "breaks" and "collisions." For the moment, let us note the permanency of the principle: antipathetic codes are "cut," made to collide, allowing the generation of extraordinary words (neologisms, for example), new messages. On the one hand, a "procedure"; on the other, utterances that would seem to inscribe themselves as if on a surface of intersecting lines.

Moreover, in defining the nature of the "redistribution" of language, Barthes advances the same principle: two heterogeneous "edges"/a cut:

Now, *such redistribution is always achieved by cutting.* Two edges are created: an obedient, conformist, plagiarizing edge . . . and *another edge*, mobile, blank (ready to assume any contours), which is never anything but the site of its effect: the place where the death of language is glimpsed. These two edges, *the compromise they bring about*, are necessary. Neither culture nor its destruction is erotic; it is the seam between them, the fault, the flaw which becomes so. *(PT, 6–7)*

This time the procedure turns into a (judicial) proceeding, — a "trial": the trial of an (obedient, conformist, plagiarizing) "edge" by another (mobile, blank); and a process, as well, that leads to a reactivation of language through the production of an intermediary *neutral* (in a sense to be redefined) textual space that subverts all canonical oppositions. Therefore, it should not be surprising that this operation is *necessary*: on the obedient "side," there is culture, the stereotypes, or stupidity — in a word, the Worn Refrain; on the other, there is as yet no speech. On one "side," the "arrogance" of victory speeches: Science, *Doxa*, triumphant Political Discourse, for example; on the other, the nothing (of pleasure), the silence or muteness (of bliss), the absence of words *(RB,* 47). The "revolution" and not the simple destruction of the (bourgeois) good conscience regarding language has a price: finding the means to "stage" a "compromise" that permits the *infans* (empty or contourless) edge to "speak" by "cutting" this nothing, this blank, with existing languages, by giving voice to this "edge" through letting all the possible languages ramble and drift through the text, two by two *(RB,* 62). This movement makes for the specificity of the "works of our modernity" and permits the following description:

Whence, perhaps, a means of evaluating the works of our modernity: their value would proceed from their duplicity. By which it must be understood that they always have two edges. The subversive edge may seem privileged because it is the edge of violence; but it is not violence which affects pleasure, nor is it destruction which interests it; what pleasure wants is the site of a loss, the seam, the cut, the deflation, the *dissolve* which seizes the subject in the midst of bliss. Culture thus recurs as an edge: in no matter what form. *(PT,* 7)

There is yet another formal trait shared by text operators. All refer to a *distributional* and *non-integrative* mode of engendering the "objects," words, and figures of the text *(LDF,* 7). No "edge" of a text ever constitutes a closed system of hierarchized elements (sentences, semes organized around a center or a principle); it always refers to a series of sentences, words, or objects. And in this way, like the lover who "speaks in bundles of sentences but does not integrate these sentences on a higher level, into a work" *(LDF,* 7), the essayist writes, so to speak, in bundles of words, through a heaping-up of objects, by juxtaposing images or by multiplying points of view. And this gives the impression that connections are lacking: within the fragments, within the work. But meanwhile we have definitively left the domain of classical *Teknè Rhétorikè*: if the essayist "reasons," it is by a "series of metaphors" (*RB*, 152); if he argues, it is by the "unfolding of an image" (ibid.). At this level and according to a progressively emerging logic, it is always the "word that leads the idea."

> One might call "poetic" (without value judgment) any discourse in which the word leads the idea: if you like words to the point of succumbing to them, you exclude yourself from the law of the signified, from *écrivance*. (*RB*, 152)

In this sense, the essayist is that writer who assumes the right and the power to succumb to desired words and to begin writing from them. Here, it is not only "parataxis" (the rupture of composition and subordination) that governs, but also a sort of generalized metonymy: words constantly replace other words, words constantly are added to each other without any finality having precedence over them:

> Michelet "eats" History; hence he "grazes" on it; hence he "walks" in it, etc.: everything that happens to an animal put out to pasture will thus be *applied* to Michelet: the metaphoric application will play the part of an explanation. (ibid.)

We have apparently come back to the domain of the *association of ideas* or "poetic license" dear to a certain type of Montaigne commentator. If the Essay as a reflective text is never constituted by a single "edge" but by at least two, one must envision a logic far more complex in order to understand what is happening. If each "edge" refers to a specific series of words or objects, what can be the nature of a Text constituted by always "cutting" at least two antipathetic codes, so as to bring at least two series of heterogeneous words and objects[32] into contact without degenerating into "cacophony"?

The "structure" of the Essay such as Barthes invents it (reinvents and interprets it) "after" Montaigne is a novel response to such a question.

5. The Problem of the Essayistic Text's "Constitution"

> The notion of the strong system: one should undoubtedly make a serious inquiry into that. (Barthes, *PRB*, 317)

> Fourier perhaps enables us to restate the following opposition (which we lately stated by distinguishing the novelistic from the novel, poetry from the poem, the essay from the dissertation, the writing from the style, production from the product, structuration from the structure): the *system* is a body of doctrine within which the elements (principles,

facts, consequences) develop logically, i.e., from the point of view of
the discourse, rhetorically. . . .

Systematics is the play of the system; it is language that is open, infinite, free from any referential illusion (pretension); its mode of appearance, its constitution, is not "development" but pulverization, dissemination (the gold dust of the signifier). (SFL, 109-110)

System / systematics. Is it not characteristic of reality to be unmaster-
able? And is it not the characteristic of any system to master it? What
then, confronting reality, can one do who rejects mastery? Get rid of
the system as apparatus, accept systematics as writing (as Fourier did).
(RB, 172)

As a reflective text, the Essay always raises at least three types of questions that
combine into a system: the topical question of its organization (which form?); the
economic question of its utterances (which thought?); and finally the dynamic
problem of its efficacy (what type of effects?). Whenever the question of its organization as constituted text is posed, the same kinds of problems appear: the
logical problem of its apparent incompletion compared to the closure of system;
the rhetorical problem of its constitution compared to the composed text. These
two problems are obviously linked and, in turn, raise a new question: that of the
general economy of the essayistic text insofar as it constitutes a work and insofar
as it exercises a certain operatory power. Moreoever, this is what justifies the
everlasting demarcation that the Essay must draw in regard to the rhetorical norm
of compositio and in regard to the logical and gnoseological norm of the system.
From a theoretical point of view, one can begin to discern more and more clearly
that the notions of rhetorical composition and of system are closely linked to the
idea of mastery.

As a matter of fact, rhetorical composition is historically justified by the double economy imposed upon it: the limited mnemic and synoptic powers of the human mind. As Jean-Louis Galay so clearly demonstrated from the point of view
of compositio: "A thing is easily known (eumathês) because it is easily retained
(eumnêmôneutos) and easily retained because it is likely to be taken in at a single
glance (eusunoptos)."[33] Consequently, the more fully a work satisfies these three
joint principles—knowable, retainable, and capable of being taken in at a single
glance with little effort—the greater will be its coherence and power. But most
important is that this art of mnemic and synoptic economy is itself inextricably
linked to the idea of mastery: there is more than a superficial relationship between
the rhetorical disposition of the elements of a text and Knowledge.

Insofar as it brings the work into accord with the memory that one has of it
and consequently with the knowledge one draws from it, "rhetorical economy,"
as Galay goes on to say, "has as its goal the exercise through knowledge of its
powers of mastery." In the philosophical tradition, this type of presentation of

ideas, having as *têlos* a project of mastery, bears the name *system*. Therefore, it comes as no surprise that Barthes dismisses in the same text both philosophic system and rhetorical composition. As an essayist, Barthes refuses any idea of mastery; therefore, he must reject, by the same token, both the notion of system and the classical norms of textual composition. Indeed, if the Essay sought mastery over a given object of Knowledge, it would essentially be obliged to depend on the various rhetorical procedures — on the one hand, the norms governing the order and composition of the major parts of the text and those governing arrangement (*taxis*) and connection (*sunthesis*) in the presentation of ideas; and on the other hand the different sites (*topoi*) stemming from the Invention and Memory of rhetoric: the commonplaces; the encyclopedia or *speculum*; the examination of layouts or plans (of house, palace, city); and, finally, the images springing from rhetorical mnemotechnics.[34] But since the Essay is defined neither as system nor as dissertation, one is necessarily led to the invention of a new economy of text and to the reinterpretation of the idea of the "work." Once the necessary link between the Essay's interest in producing knowledge (its specific effects) and the notion of mastery is questioned, one must have recourse to another conception of the text in order to understand what takes place.

Like the "fragmental text" in general, the Essay gives the impression of deficiency at the level of the rhetorical relations that generally constitute the work as a continuous text. Barthes aptly comments: "I do not know how to reproduce the 'masses'." But one must not be misled: when one defines the Essay negatively or privatively as an unconstituted, incomplete, chaotic, etc., text, one only resuscitates tacitly the illusion that historically has assimilated the notion of the work "to the practice — followed by the majority — in which the text is endowed with a *compositional* unity."[35] Therefore, it is necessary to reformulate the questions in other terms: can a text whose ideal of writing is to contest the rules of rhetoric still constitute a *work*? Valéry's answers to such a question are well known. The first consists in the always renewed, but never realized project tending toward a type of composition that is increasingly rigorous and demanding, committing the work to the goal of an absolute summa. The second consists in renouncing from the start all composition, or more precisely, renouncing everything in the composition destined to produce the appearance of textual continuity ("the bloc effect.") Here are asserted the deliberate decision to fragment the text and the definitive renunciation of the sort of expository synthesis that rhetoric has imposed. When Barthes says that he does not know how to "reproduce the masses," he makes the same type of commitment. But, this said, the Barthesian Essay collects its pieces and fragments according to completely different sets of relations.

Although not "composed" on a strictly rhetorical plane, the Barthesian Essay is nonetheless a *constituted* text on the formal plane. But beside the synthesis offered by rhetoric, beside the philosophical system ("closed," "monosemic," and "dogmatic"), there remains for one who has renounced mastery the possibility of system as *procedure*. Procedure as the opening out of structure into structuration allows the Essay to invent a new space of writing and reading.

> This procedure is a constant one: he rarely starts from the idea in order to invent an image for it subsequently; he starts from a sensuous object, and then hopes to meet in his work with the possibility of finding an *abstraction* for it, levied on the intellectual culture of the moment. (*RB*, 99)

> This is a constant procedure in your work: you use a pseudo-linguistics, a metaphorical linguistics: not that grammatical concepts seek out images in order to express themselves, but just the contrary, because these concepts come to constitute allegories, a second language, whose abstraction is diverted to fictive ends: the most serious of the sciences, the one which is responsible for the very being of language and supplies a whole portion of austere names, is *also* a reservoir of images, and as a poetic language enables you to utter what is strictly your desire. (*RB*, 124)

Procedure is the essayist's *tactical* response to the problem of the text's "*constitution*." Procedure is opposed to rhetorical composition and philosophical system from several points of view:

(1) by the mode of appearance and constitution of the objects it allows one to produce: in this text, neither "development" nor "plan" takes precedence, but rather the pulverization, the dissemination of signifiers. As Barthes notes, "no voice (Science, Cause, Institution) is *behind* what it is saying" (*PT*, 30). It has liquidated all metalanguage: the connections are missing.

(2) by the type of discourse it engenders: this discourse is without *object* ("it only speaks of a thing obliquely, by approaching it indirectly" [*SFL*, 110]), and without *subject* (here, the author " 'performs' his enunciatory role in such a manner that we cannot decide whether it is serious or parody" [*SFL*, 110]). Thus, it destroys all the discursive categories where one would be tempted to place it: genres, types, modes. As Barthes says, this is the Text's model: "It is 'the comical that does not make us laugh,' the irony which does not subjugate, the jubilation without soul, without mystique, . . . quotation without quotation marks" (*PT*, 30–31).

(3) by the type of operations it conditions: it is a "vast madness which does not end, but which permutates" (*SFL*, 110), couples, disassociates, etc.

(4) by the type of uses it defines: like systematics, procedure "is not concerned with application" (of a knowledge, a meaning, etc.), but "with transmission, (significant) circulation" (*SFL*, 110).

(5) Finally, by the quality of language it produces: "language that is open, infinite, free from any referential illusion (pretension)" (*SFL*, 110). At this level, it is the license taken by procedure with regard to the canonical structures of lan-

guage itself that is important: the lexicon is renewed (exuberant neologisms, portmanteau words, transliterations, etc.), syntax disrupted ("no more logical cell, no more 'sentence' in the classical sense of the term").

In any case, these five determinations[36] are only "fallout," effects of the implementation of procedure. While they characterize certain of its properties, they still do not permit the original nature of the Barthesian Essay to be grasped.

From a formal point of view, procedure designates at least three distinct things that define a very specific type of structure:

(1) *Generalized*, procedure first of all designates a certain treatment of words, texts, objects, languages in an open intertextual space.

One word describes this order and this treatment of "*language-substance*" (*PT*, 31), when it is the object of procedure: *paragrammatics* as mobilization through the writing of an order and its opposite, of an image and its opposite, or more generally as the "superimpression (in dual hearing) of two languages that are ordinarily foreclosed to each other" (*SFL*, 93).

(2) *Qualified*, procedure also designates a "method" systematically implemented in order to obtain a certain result: at this level, it characterizes the Essay as an "art of effects."

This is the site of those "felicities of expression," "inspired finds," "charms," and "apt turns of phrase" that have the ring of truth for us and make us say of such and such a figure, "Yes, that's it, that's really it."

(3) *Specified* with regard to the logic of the system, procedure designates the different forms assumed by the unfolding of a process of textual production: spiral, slant, zig-zag, swivel, and an entire series of "secondary" formal procedures engendered by the principal procedure.

Consequently, the source of the essayistic form's specificity can be clearly traced: it is the heterogeneity of the principles and forms that procedure implements in order to produce its utterances that explains the heterogeneity and the multiplicity of qualifications and *therefore of forms* that an Essay can *integrate* without degenerating into cacophony.

When Montaigne says that his *Essays* are sometimes a "fricassée," sometimes an "entanglement" or a "rhapsody," when Barthes describes his "self-portrait" as "some Valenciennes lace," a "patchwork made from badly put together squares," a "Moroccan wadi," or a "broken television screen," it is clearly in a metaphorical sense, but it is also, above all, a direct reference to the diversity and the multiplicity of "tones" and "registers" produced and made to coexist by the procedure.

In any case, this should not be taken as merely a "manner of speaking": like a "banquette," a "faceted cube," or a "Japanese stew" (*RB*, 74), the Essay refers to the multiple resources and the *power* of procedure as a new system of production and constitution of a text which produces *its* rhetoric at the same time as it engenders its utterances. Just as the poet can say: to each text its own rhetoric (Francis Ponge), so the essayist can say: to each fragment its own form, its own rhetoric, and its own mode of engendering. This is to say, finally, that like a "layered pastry," "onion," or "braid" (*RB*, 74), the Essay always refers to procedure as the operator that makes possible a text which is *all this at once* and can still be many other things: a harmonious hodgepodge, the freely inventive design of a patchwork quilt, a metaphoric linguistics, a pseudo-philosophy, and more.

But even in view of this, a certain number of questions remain: what, then, gives a certain *unity* in spite of everything, to this deliberate multiplicity? What, then, makes a certain *Totality* of these heterogeneous and scattered fragments? In short, what gives the Essay, in spite of all this, a specific Unity and Totality?

These questions are foreign to philosophical discourse, which seeks to confine literature to System's projected mastery and rhetorical closure,[37] but they are familiar ones for the Essay and a certain number of texts that share with it a liking for procedures and for complication (of genres, of words). Indeed, when Malcolm Lowry says of his novel *Under the Volcano*, in the preface to the French edition, "It can be regarded as a sort of symphony, opera, or even a western," when he says that he wanted to make it into "jazz, a poem, a song, a tragedy, a comedy, a farce *and so on*," one cannot help but be struck by the analogies that exist between this cascade of qualifiers and those found by Montaigne or Barthes to name what they do. But still more striking is Lowry's view of the mode of functioning and the specific unity of his "novel." Lowry writes: "It can be thought of as a *sort of machine*: it works, make no mistake about it, as I discovered at my expense. And in case you think that I made anything but a novel out of it, I want to tell you that when it comes right down to it, I wanted to write a genuine novel, even a damned serious novel."[38]

And this is perhaps the most that can be said at this point concerning the problem of unity in the essayistic text: it works, it functions (make no mistake about it), as we can find out at our own expense. It has been written, certainly, at the expense of the "author." But lest we think that the essayist can write *anything, no matter what*, she, like the novelist, will tell us that she wanted to write a genuine text, and even a damned serious one. And even though the essayist no longer has the guard-rails of concept and system at hand, she can rely on the *efficacy of a complex machine*, one whose cogwheels must now be dismantled one by one.

6. The Structural Reflex

Then if you put the fragments one after the next, is no organization possible? Yes: the fragment is like the musical idea of a song cycle: each piece is self-sufficient, and yet it is never anything but the interstice of its neighbors: the work consists of no more than an inset, an *hors-texte*. The man who has best understood and practiced the aesthetic of the fragment (before Webern) is perhaps Schumann . . . everything he produced was ultimately *intercalated* but between what and what? What is the meaning of a pure series of interruptions? (*RB*, 94)

Who is still a structuralist? Yet he is one in this, at least: a uniformly noisy place seems to him unstructured because in this place there is no freedom left to choose silence or speech. . . . . Structure at least affords me two terms, one of which I can deliberately choose and the other dismiss: hence it is on the whole a (modest) pledge of freedom. (*RB*, 117)

Sometimes it happens that language itself provides the bifurcation of a double word: "structure," a positive value initially, has come to be discredited when it was apparent that too many people conceived it as a motionless form (a "blueprint," a "schema," a "model"); luckily "structuration" was there to take up the slack, implying the positive value par excellence; the *praxis*, the perverse expenditure ("for nothing"). (*RB*, 62)

Barthes does not elude the difficulties raised by the organization of the fragmental text: "What is the meaning of a *pure* series of interruptions?" he asks. This not only shows that he is perfectly conscious of the problem, but also confirms unambiguously that, from start to finish in an Essay, fragments remain fragments. At this level, "parataxis" reigns. Where is the organization then? Clearly, the answer to such a question is found neither in philosophical system nor in Rhetoric: this would be to think that an Essay can be summarized or arranged otherwise; this would be to believe that the engendering of its utterances obeys a modality of production extrinsic or external to its content, an "immobile form": a preexisting plan, schema or model. But such is not the case: if an Essay cannot be summarized or translated into terms other than those it *presents*, it is because the procedure at the origin of its "objects" designates less a form than an *activity*, less a structure than a *structuration*. Montaigne points this out when he writes: "My book and I are one." Here the book cannot be separated from its creator. Barthes notes this by insisting on the "constancy" of the "procedure" he uses: thanks to procedure, "no more anguish of 'schema,' no more rhetoric of 'development,' no more twisted logic, no more dissertations! *An idea per fragment, a fragment per idea* . . . " (*RB*, 147, emphasis mine).

In order to understand the very special type of unity and totality to which the Barthesian essay refers, we must start from "procedure." But it must be noted that procedure (1) does not function in just any condition, and (2) does not define just any unity or totality. In fact, for a procedure to be effective, certain very special formal conditions must exist. (The author's "genius" and "originality" constitute a completely superimposed and separate ingredient that cannot be taken into account here.)

Procedure must be employed with faultless rigor and constancy if the Essay is not to explode into informal notations and if it is to constitute an integral work in its own right. More precisely, if procedure is an instrument that produces the essay as an integral work of literature in its own right—that is, in accordance with the category in which I am trying to rethink its economy and redefine its efficacy here, as a *reflective text*—this is primarily because of its *organization in series*. This implies first the existence of at least two heterogeneous series of words or objects, or two series of events; or two series of propositions; or two series of meanings or expressions.[39] These variations are not crucial: the essential thing, as we have already seen, is the heterogeneity of the series ("classes" as Barthes says), the duality or the antagonism of two codes, of two antipathetic edges, and an irreducible difference between them, the existence of a "gap" between them that no word, no concept can saturate.

But procedure implies a *second fundamental trait*: the two series of objects or words, the two edges of the text it complicates must not be "equal"; in other words, they cannot have the same value or valence. In fact, one series will always be considered as *signifying* and the other as *signified*: there will always be a natural *excess* in the signifying series and a natural *lack* in the signified series. As Deleuze says: "One has to understand at the same time that the two series are *marked*, one by excess, the other by lack, and that the *two determinations trade places without ever balancing each other*" (*Logique du sens*, 65).

Therefore, what is in excess for example in the signifying series of sensuous objects as a series of likes and dislikes, is literally an empty space, a place without occupant, that always moves about like a ferret: namely, the body as a *floating signifier*. In other words, this is a series of objects marked by the general valence of "plus" or "minus": "*I like, I don't like*" (*RB*, 117, and *CL*, 27).

Conversely, what is lacking in the *signified* series of *intellectual objects* borrowed from the "culture of the moment" is always the body as mana-word, but this time no longer as an empty space, a place without occupant, but rather as a "supernumerary given, not placed, unknown, an occupant without place and always displaced" (Deleuze, ibid., 65). In other words, the body once more but as a *floated signified* in search of an object or as an embryonic subject in search of an identity, or finally as a divided passive self in search of a place in the tableau of possibilities.[40]

The very special nature of series is such that there is always a signifier in excess in the signifying series of "sensual objects" and simultaneously always a signified lacking in the series of "intellectual objects" that resonate with them. In this way, "procedure" never consists simply in naming or qualifying one series by the other, or in collapsing the two according to a relation of expression, representation, or analogy. For example, there is no resemblance, no semantic affinity at the outset between Tokyo (the city, the word) and the "Lacanian subject," no immediate or obvious analogy between Morocco and the structure of the French language, no tie, no "natural" passage between Nicaraguan soldiers and the nuns (*CL*, 42). Only the body as mana-word — that is to say, as irreducible difference and atopic principle of all structuration — or as *paradoxical object* makes possible such a term-for-term telescoping of two series; only the body allows the complication of their respective differences.

What "procedure" designates, therefore, is not the *resemblance* between the primary heterogeneous series, and even less is it their initial or final identity. What "procedure" designates is, above all, the power of the mana-word as the "dark precursor" (Deleuze) of always dissimilar and unequal series that become increasingly remote and different — and perhaps it would be better to say *différant* here. As Barthes so aptly puts it: "We need unbridled pluralism." For "one touch of difference leads to racism. But a great deal of difference leads away from it, irremediably." (*RB*, 69).

Like Montaigne with his "sufficient word" (*mot-bastant*),[41] Barthes does not rely on the mana-word "body" to designate a first or a final signified; the essential function of the mana-word is to express a "primary intensity" as pure difference that always puts (at least) two heterogeneous series into contact: the first, "signifying," that refers to "sensuous objects" always in excess, and that defines the edge of the "blank, mobile" desire that is "ready to assume any contour": always constituted by gestures, emotions, "flushes of pleasure," fears, phantasms, likes and dislikes. And this is the moment of "gestures of the idea." The second, "signified," and that refers this time to "intellectual objects," always lacking, defining the "obedient, conformist, plagiarizing edge" (*PT*, 6). This is the moment of conversion and/or convulsion of value into Theory. The essential thing is never to take this opposition at face value, never to honor it too quickly, to play as long as possible the game of differences that the mana-word makes possible. This complex movement of profusion and dissemination has a name in Barthes's works: it is called (having) the "structural reflex":

> The structural reflex consists in deferring the pure difference as long as
> possible to the end of a common stem: so that the meaning explode,
> pure and clear, *in extremis*: so that the victory of meaning be won in
> the nick of time, as in a good thriller. (*RB*, 153)

I shall return a little later to the meaning of this necessary and *in extremis* "explosion" of meaning. What clearly appears now is that "procedure" no longer aims at the unity of a system of thoughts or ideas; in the image of the mana-word, it also must be multiform and diverse: like the mana-word, it must assure the circulation of differences from one end of the text to the other, respect the "spacing-out of languages," in brief, be the instrument of the fundamental "duplicity" of all genuine "value" and the means of multiplying possible discourses. This is why it is always accompanied by secondary figures or rather, this is why it splits into an *indefinite* variety of new procedures: sometimes a *straight line*, and sometimes a *zig-zag* or a form that combines these two figures simultaneously: for example, a *spiral* or *swivel*, the children's game of *topping hands*, or a *layered pastry*. Thus, it assures a minimum of "continuity" in the work.[42]

7. The Essay as an Intensive System

Alongside the different modalities of rhetorical composition and in opposition to the synthetic and extensive system of philosophy, a "system" of a completely different nature becomes conceivable with the Essay. Thanks to Deleuze's works on the notion of "intensive system," today we have a precise knowledge of certain qualities of this type of "system."[43]

When by some "procedure" a "coupling" is established between two heterogeneous series of "objects" around a given paradoxical word, there automatically results (1) an "internal resonance" in the system from which is derived (2) a "forced movement" whose amplitude goes beyond the base series themselves. As Deleuze says:

> When communication is established between the heterogeneous series, all sorts of consequences follow within the system. Something "crosses" *between the edges*; events *explode*, phenomena flash like lightning or thunder. Time/space dynamisms fill the system, expressing both the resonance of the coupled pairs of the series and the amplitude of the forced movement that spills beyond them. The system is peopled by subjects, at once embryonic subjects, and passive egos. (Deleuze, *Différence et répétition*, 155)

One might object that this type of "system" is not especially literary and that Deleuze has recourse to concepts in physics in order to define the different qualities. But in fact, one must not have preconceptions about the "qualification" of such "systems": mechanical, physical, biological, social, philosophical, or "literary." No doubt each type of "system" has specific conditions of effectuation, but this is not the problem: what one must prove is that the Essay as text also conforms to the same principles; what one must attempt to reveal is the nature of the "structuration" it implements in order to function.

Gilles Deleuze was able to show that in works as diverse as those by Roussel, Proust, Joyce, or Gombrowicz the same "system" was operative: namely, the implementation of "a very special procedure," as Roussel says,[44] that allows the production of an infinity of words, the generation of an infinity of stories from a given atopic "linguistic precursor"—homonymous or quasi-homonymous (Pillard-Billard) in Roussel, esoteric words or portmanteau words in Joyce, the "precious image" in Proust—in short, verbal series, always, that an esoteric word couples or ramifies to infinity.

As "intensive system" or reflective text, the Essay clearly resorts to quite different preconditions—in other words, it possesses its own "operality" (Jean-Louis Galay)—but they can all be traced to the structural characteristics of the system that I have tried to define, following Deleuze. In such a "system," one always proceeds from at least two primary unequal and divergent series—two "antipathetic edges," as Barthes says (*PT*, 6–7)—coupled through a procedure around a "value-word" that complicates their respective differences. But as we know, each time that a coupling of this type takes place, an "internal resonance" occurs in the "system"—the *text*. In the Barthesian Essay, this "internal resonance" always takes two distinct forms:

(1) The form of a "pensive sonority," or as Barthes says, a "song of sentence-ideas" or, again, a "music of figures, metaphors, thought-words" (*RB*, 107, 145), at the level of *minimal unities* of the "system," which are puns, amphibologies, enantiosemes, etc. What happens here in the system, between the resonating series of sensual objects and intellectual objects under the action of the mana-word as linguistic precursor conditioning their couplage, is called "a gesture of the idea" or "allegory,"[45] but in a completely new sense. All these "preciously ambiguous" words, all these baroque neologisms, all these telescopings of signifiers or objects, in short all these "felicities of expression"—"light, diffuse, and mercurial," as Barthes calls them—traverse the Essay whenever, thanks to the power of the "system," a concept in a given series is coupled with one in another series or a word is "split"[46] in two in a carnivalesque manner, but also each time that one code or language is set aslant by another.

In the notions of allegory, of the word as "gesture of the idea," or of the *object* as "sensual" or "intellectual" object, there is something very similar to what happens in Joyce's "epiphanies" or Proust's "precious images." In each case, the same system of resonance between heterogeneous series is operative: by making two objects resonate, Proust produces a "precious image" and James Joyce an "epiphany," whereas Barthes produces the word as gesture of the idea or as allegory. In this sense, allegory is not simple polysemy (the "multiple of meaning"), but meaning as "duplicity," word as *gesture*, image as phantasm, "figure" as *schêma*, "the body's gesture caught in action," or "operatic aria" (*LDF*, 4–5).

The system is what provides the chance or "favorable disposition" that permits the ambiguity that lies in the words to be *actualized*, and that also, most of the time, permits new ambiguities, new words to be produced, thus renewing the lexicon.

(2) The form, also, of a "doctrinal vibration" (*RB*, 74) or of the "musical idea of a song cycle" (*RB*, 94) but this time at the level of those *units of higher rank*, the fragments of the Essay as partial textual objects impossible to totalize, primordial pieces that do not refer to any prior entity: "each piece is self-sufficient," as

Barthes says. Little pictures, lexias, titled paragraphs, partitioned-off scenes that do not communicate directly with each other, *numen* and "framed" poses, descriptions or maxims that come to a sudden end, short narratives, anamneses, and so on. The very essence of the fragment is to be self-sufficient; its economy, its method belongs to *torin* Buddhism: "a method of abrupt, separated, broken openings" (*RB*, 94). One looks in vain to Barthes for clichés about the work as an organic totality in which the whole determines the part, and in which each part predetermines the whole (a rhetorical and dialectical conception of the work as closure). This is why the fragments are so resistant to any transformation: to summing up, contraction, or translation into another narrative or another discourse. In fact, implying as it does an economy of immediate bliss, the fragment does not like endings, developments: " 'Development' would be countered by 'tone,' something articulated and sung, a diction: here it is *timbre* which should reign" (*RB*, 94). Not destined to be integrated into a totality, the fragments do not succeed each other any more than they complete each other: "What is the meaning of a pure series of interruptions?" (ibid.).

Here also only the *formal* structure of the work enables the fragment to be deciphered not as part of a whole, and even less as the "germ" of an organic totality,[47] but as an "intercalated" piece in a cycle: *intermezzo*, a pure resonance between *intermezzi*:

He [Schumann] called the fragment an "intermezzo"; he increased the intermezzi within his works as he went on composing: everything he produced was ultimately *intercalated*: but between what and what?" (ibid.)

"Between what and what?" As we see, even the essayist succumbs to the "rhetorical clausule." We know, indeed, that a play, a scene, or a fragment of an Essay need not be in a given place for a certain continuity to "be understood" in the heteroclitic succession where they are inserted: the intensive system creates this ideal of "a high condensation, not of thought, or of wisdom, or of truth . . . but of music" (*RB*, 94), that assures the exchange between the most heterogeneous fragments and produces the internal solidarity specific to each essay.

Though it is satisfying enough in broad terms, such an analysis is nevertheless in error on at least one point: it leads one to think that "allegory" and, generally, all the "preciously ambiguous" words that traverse the Essay are merely "samples"—what Barthes calls "miniatures" or elements *subordinate* to the fragment. From this perspective, the fragment is conceived as a simple *sum* of "allegories." Worse yet: no status is given to the economy of the latter as "details." But a close reading of those texts in which Barthes approaches this question shows that it is absolutely impossible to assimilate fragment and *detail* without another form of process. In the pages that follow, I would like to analyze this delicate problem in greater depth.

8. The "Third Meaning"

But we also have a body of bliss consisting solely of erotic relations, utterly distinct from the first body; it is another contour, another nomination; thus with the text: it is no more than the open list of the fires of language (those living fires, intermittent lights, wandering features strewn in the text like seeds and which for us advantageously replace the "*semina aeternitatis*," the "*zopyra*," the common notions, the fundamental assumptions of ancient philosophy). (*PT*, 16–17)

Why this curiosity about petty details: schedules, habits, meals, lodging, clothing, etc.? Is it the hallucinatory relish of "reality" (the very materiality of "*that once existed*")? And is it not the fantasy itself which invokes the "detail," the tiny private scene, in which I can easily take my place? (*PT*, 53)

In this habitually unary space, occasionally (but alas all too rarely) a "detail" attracts me. I feel that its mere presence changes my reading, that I am looking at a new photograph, marked in my eyes with a higher value. This "detail" is the *punctum*. (*CL*, 42)

Here then are three texts deliberately taken from different contexts where the notion of "detail" could not have been more clearly "isolated" by Barthes. Is this merely by chance? In a more solemn and intimate text, Barthes examines the same subject more closely: "Were I a writer, and dead, how I would love it if my life, through the pains of some friendly and detached biographer, were to reduce itself to *a few details*, a few preferences, a few inflections, let us say: to "biographemes" whose distinction and mobility might go beyond any fate and come to touch, *like Epicurean atoms*, some future body, destined to the same dispersion" (*SFL*, 9, emphasis mine).

It is even more striking that when, in another connection, Barthes speaks directly of his manner of "composing," he again insists on the difference between the "detail" and the "fragment": "In other words," he writes in *Roland Barthes*, I proceed by addition, not by sketch; I have the antecedent (initial) taste for the detail, the fragment, the *rush*" (*RB*, 94). And when, elsewhere, Barthes writes, "Reading a text cited by Stendhal . . . I find Proust in one minute detail" (*PT*, 35) or when he writes that he "naively connects detail to detail" when he attempts to copy a drawing (*RB*, 93), we ought to admit that we are confronted with an entity that is utterly inassimilable without mediation to the fragment or to the language scene in which it is embedded.[48]

As "language fireworks," a "meandering trace," "seed," "miniscule scene," or "allegory," the *detail* belongs to quite another "cutting up" of the text than does the fragment. Hence the necessity to distinguish "detail" and "fragment" carefully and to elucidate the nature of their relation(s): this problem is at the heart of the question of the "genre" of the Essay as a specific fragmental text.

As is the case with other theoretical questions for Barthes, the problem of the economy of exchanges between "detail" and "fragment" is confronted head-on, not in a consideration of the theory of literature, but in a book devoted to film. Indeed, in a very fine essay "The Third Meaning" (*TM*, 52–68), Barthes examines a question of the same genre: that of the status of the single frame (*le photogramme*) in relation to the complete shot (*plan*) in Eisenstein's films. In this regard, there are striking analogies between what I am attempting to formulate here about "detail" and what Eisenstein said concerning the new cinematic possibilities offered by *montage*. Discussing the links between image (frame/photogram) and shot (as cinematographic "fragment"), Eisenstein wrote: "The basic centre of gravity . . . is transferred to *inside* the fragment, into the elements included in the image itself. And the centre of gravity is no longer the element 'between shots'—the 'shock'—but the element 'inside the shot'—the accentuation within the fragment." (Eisenstein, quoted by Barthes, ibid., 67)

We have already encountered this "language scene": "Cut off" from its neighbors, and, moreover, causing parataxis to reign supreme at its very center, the fragment is not defined by its position in a compositional chain: it is, as Barthes says, "syntagmatically irresponsible." Therefore, we are not dealing with a simple analogy but rather with an object of the same essence. Like the cinematographic fragment that the filmmaker edits after the fact (*après-coup*), the essayistic fragment is "subject in its very structure to asyndeton and anacoluthon, figures of interruption and short-circuiting" (*RB*, 93). This is how we could account for the elements of a higher rank in the Essay: fragments, lexias, paragraphs, little pictures, etc.

But still more troubling is the fact that a phenomenon of the same order occurs at the level of these "scattered seeds"—nontotalizable—that are the details in an essay. Actually, here more than one analogy can be drawn between the "detail" ("linguistic allegory" or *punctum*) and what Barthes earlier suggested we consider under the category of "obtuse sense." First, like obtuse sense, the "detail" is discontinuous, indifferent to all narrative (*récit*) and generally to every "obvious" meaning (*sens obvie*). Never outside of the Essay's discourse, never outside its formal internal organization, could the "Lacanian subject" be considered spontaneously as an equivalent for Tokyo, for example. Outside of the procedure that produces it out of whole cloth, it has, so to speak, no "objective" existence; a "semantologist" would not readily acknowledge its existence. With respect to the "real" as "nature" (a "realist" instance), the "detail" *as the obtuse sense of the fragment* is the mark of a radical rupture with regard to any "concrete" referent: it is rather a "leaning on the signifier" or, if you prefer, "the signifier as siren" (*RB*, 145). Barthes fully accepted this "im-pertinence" of "detail" as "punctuation" (*punctum*)—"*Punctum* is also: sting, speck, cut, little hole" (*CL*, 27).—when he writes: "One might call "poetic" (without value judgment) any discourse in which the word leads the idea: if you like words to the point of succumbing to them, you exclude yourself from the law of the signified" (*RB*, 152).

But the parallel between the two instances I am discussing does not stop here. Like "obtuse sense" or inarticulable "punctum," the detail "does not fill up." You could say that "it is in a permanent state of *depletion*" (*TM*, 62). At this point, we know in what sense: in fact, at once floating signifier (Tokyo) and floated signified (Lacanian subject), it "maintains a state of perpetual erethism, desire not finding issue in that spasm of the signified which normally brings the subject voluptuously back into the peace of nominations" (ibid.).

Finally, if the "detail" can be interpreted as "accent," "pensive sonority," or "music of thought-words," it is also "the very form of an emergence, of a fold (a crease even), marking the heavy layer of informations and signification" — or, like the Japanese haiku, "an anaphoric gesture without significant content, a sort of gash rased of meaning (ibid.). It is not surprising that Barthes gives this definition of the haiku in a fragment entitled "Movement of objects into discourse": "Thus, sometimes, in Japanese haiku, the line of written words suddenly opens and there is the drawing of Mount Fuji or of a sardine which delicately appears in place of the abandoned word" (*RB*, 135).

These characteristics explain why I omitted the haiku from the list of syntagmas of a higher rank in the Essay: whereas despite everything there may arise within the fragment some hint of narrative or condensed argument — even if only in the form of the "unfolding of an image" — like the haiku, the "detail" is the "counter-narrative; disseminated, reversible, set to its own temporality" (*TM*, 63) that no "anecdote" can sum up, that no concept can subsume.[49] This also explains the diversity and the heterogeneity of the textual operators and procedures that are put into play in an Essay: the dominant figure that governs the formation of fragments is indisputably that of *complication* (the diagonal encounter of several languages, the montage of different texts, the telescopings of quotations from various sources, etc.). But the figure that governs the formation of "allegories" is *implication*: words of double meaning, enantiosemes, amphibologies, etc.

It is only by taking into account the double economy controlling elements of different magnitudes that one can understand the type of "resonance" which they induce in the "system" and the novel kind of unity they give the Essay as reflective text. The intrusion of "detail," of the "miniscule scene," of the haiku of "allegory," and so forth into the essayistic text profoundly reshapes the theoretical status of the fragment, and consequently the classical conception of the work as a "composed" text. An altogether unprecedented displacement occurs at the very heart of the traditional "reading" of the Essay as a discontinuous text.

As an *irreducible* piece, the detail can no longer be considered as a remote "by-product" of the fragment, a "free sample" or an excerpt of the Essay, but rather as that which fundamentally determines the overall economy of the fragment, in short the "inside" of the fragment. And it is here that Eisenstein's reflection, which served as my point of departure, assumes its full meaning: In moving from the fragment to the "detail" as the specific entity of the Essay, one does not proceed from a "whole" to its "parts," nor does one proceed from an "organic totality" to the embryonic *semina aeternitatis* or "common notions" out of which the totality grows. With the "detail," as it functions in an Essay, the center of gravity of the Essay – as a text made up by the "montage" and "coupling" of heterogeneous series of "words" – "is transferred to *inside* the fragment, into the elements included in the image itself" (*TM*, 67). Prior to the "composition," there is thus the implication of images, of details, of miniscule scenes that envelop manifold meanings, contain innumerable objects, and *reflect* thousands of (language) fireworks. At this point, I can translate Eisenstein's comment into the terms of my own exposition: the Essay's center of gravity will no longer be the element "between fragments" – the fragment as *intermezzo* or the "shock" of fragments – but the singular image, the detail, the haiku *within the fragment*, the accentuation inside the fragment.[50]

This displacement of the essay's center of gravity, from fragment to "detail," is in fact at the origin of the double "resonance" I noted earlier. Atopic and inarticulable, the "detail" nonetheless establishes "a right to the syntagmatic disjunction of images" (*TM*, 67) that conditions a resonance of the first degree: as ACCENT, or ACCENTUATION. It is at this level that one can speak of an essayist's *style*: in reading, for example, that in judo "a man scarcely touches the ground," that Einstein's brain is an "anthological organ," or that rice gives way beneath a pair of chopsticks in an "immoderate defection,"[51] one feels something quite other than "the trace of an earth-shaking transport" (*SFL*, 90). Of these expressions – of these "charms" in the sense Valéry gave to that word – one can only say what Barthes himself wrote about the "little details" that, for him, constitute the "whole" of Fourier:

> I am carried away, dazzled, convinced by a kind of *charm* in the expression, which is its delight. Fourier is crammed full of these delights: no discourse was ever *happier*. . . . I do not resist these pleasures, they seem "true" to me: I have been "taken in" by the form. (*SFL*, 91)

Like the "true" expression in Fourier, the "detail" in Barthes (and in Montaigne as well) derives its "felicity" – its resonance and impact on us – from a kind of sudden springing up. Like Fourier's expressions, it is "eccentric, displaced, all alone beside its context," pure "felicity of expression," pure "fire of language," mercurial circulation of precious words that traverse the text and *ravish* the reader. These are some of the figures that the "detail" in an Essay implies: a succession of interlocking – as well as mocking – words, a series of enveloping meanings that collaborate in defining a completely new type of text, a completely original structuration: "a structuration *which slips away from the inside* (*TM*, 64), and perhaps it would be more accurate to say: *toward* the inside of the text.

But it is possible to carry the comparison between film frame and detail a step further: though the "detail" is not a "part" of the Essay — such a notion would assign a kind of *statistical* and *homogeneous* nature to the "elements" of the essayistic text — it can, nevertheless, like the film frame in relation to the shot or the complete film, be considered a "quotation": that is, an element that both "parodies" and "disseminates." It is this dimension that is found again in some of Barthes's other definitions of the Essay (or of the Text):

> Doom of the essay, compared to the novel: doomed to *authenticity* — to the preclusion of quotation marks. (*RB*, 89) The text destroys utterly, *to the point of contradiction*, its own discursive category. . . . It is the "comical that does not make us laugh," the irony which does not subjugate, the jubilation without soul, without mystique (Sarduy), quotation without quotation marks. (*PT*, 30–31)

It cannot be said that the Essay is a "sum" of details or allegories (in the style of those miscellaneous collections: albums, florilegia, books of exempla, and so on), nor that the "detail" is an *extract* of the Essay, for the "detail" has its own logic. A discontinuous and eccentric trait within the fragment, a parodic and disseminated trait within the Essay, the "detail" profoundly modifies the classical status of reading and its object.

(1) In place of the lexeological *continuum*, it substitutes a reading which is at once *instantaneous* (since we are set aslant at each occurrence by the "form" of the detail and "ravished" by it) and *vertical* (since from one occurrence to another, the workings of "style" are recognized). In a general way, therefore, the reading of an Essay obeys neither a logical time ("which is only an operative time") nor a chronological time (which presupposes all the artifices of *têchnê rhêtorikê*: a plan, a progression, "developments"). Rather, the reading obeys a time that invokes a completely different dimension, one that is *vertical* (i.e., transversal or, as Montaigne said, "oblique").[52]

It is this dimension which establishes the resonance of the "details" among themselves, and across the "accents" they spread through the text and the resonance, on second hearing, that prevails within and between the fragments. Without this accentuation — this "diction," or to put it better this "mirror reflection" *within each fragment* — the Essay could never make a unity out of the heterogeneity of the disparate elements that constitute it. The fragment would be atonic and the "detail" uncommunicating (without resonance). When Barthes says that "timbre" should rule within a fragment, he is referring to the ability of "details," of "allegories," etc., to refer back always — independently of their "degree of elevation," "intensity," or "duration" — to a recognizable "sonority" and "style." When he contrasts the "tone" running through his essays to "development" (*RB*, 94), he is referring to the new role of reading that the Essay establishes: reading as "traversing" through signs and writing.

(2) The presence of "detail" as a disseminating and inarticulable element provokes at the same time a mutation of the text. In fact, in place of a "composed" text, it substitutes a polyphonic and discontinuous (nondialectic) text wherein the parts communicate without totalization and where, inversely, a unity is produced without recuperating differences (and losses of meaning) and without reabsorbing the gaps between elements.[53] Finally, in this kind of text, unity and totality are no longer principles of organization, but rather oblique effects of the specific mode of production and arrangement by which the text is compounded (*RB*, 148).

In reading (analyzing) such a text one must appeal no longer to a synoptic vision but rather to a "third sense," namely, to the HEARING that Barthes himself described as "the metaphor which best suits textuality," namely, a reading of the text, but as "orchestration," "counterpoint," and "stereophony." Only a reading of this kind can keep track of the "permutative deployment" of "details" and their dissemination in the text; only such a reading allows one to render an account of, to orchestrate, the units of different magnitude, fragments and details. This reading, then, is that elevated point of view — elevated, here, in a necessarily relative sense — which puts an end to the confusion between a text that is *not rhetorically composed* and a text that is *not formally constituted*.

9. Forced Movement and Generic Conflagration

Everything seems to suggest that his discourse proceeds according to a two-term dialectic: popular opinion and its contrary, *Doxa* and its paradox, the stereotype and the novation, fatigue and freshness, relish and disgust: *I like/I don't like*. This binary dialectic is the dialectic of meaning itself (*marked/not marked*) and of the Freudian game the child plays (*Fort/Da*): the dialectic of value.

Yet is this quite true? In him, another dialectic appears, trying to find expression: the contradiction of the terms yields in his eyes by the discovery of a third term, which is not a synthesis but a *translation*: everything comes back, but it comes back as Fiction, i.e., at another turn of the spiral. (*RB*, 68–69)

As we saw earlier, a dialectic movement never comes about between the fragments and the "details" of the Essay: it is not a "synthesis" of the two that leads to the internal "resonance" which brings them into contact with each other; it is not an organic totality that makes them collaborate to form a unity *despite everything*; the "details" are not parts of the fragments and the fragments themselves are not extracts of the Essay as text. It is insofar as they — both fragments and details — refer to the mana-word complicating all of them, that they succeed in forming this unity of the manifold, the Essay. It is also to the extent that they all imply, in some degree, an object that always refers to the body as writing or quotation, that they all converge toward a totality wherein the parts subsist as such. One must not be taken in by appearances: never do the heterogeneous series of objects (of likes and dislikes), never do the series of words that one *couples* or *cuts* with other series of words, never do the "antipathetic" or dual codes that enter into resonance under the influence of a value-word define a "dialectic."

Yet it is true that one always proceeds from a binary opposition and that, consequently, the essayist's discourse *seems* to function according to a dialectical movement, just as the discourse of Montaigne's *Essays* seems to "be tossed in the wind." But we now know that the opposition—whatever form it may assume: antithesis, *Adhomination*, contradiction, and so on—is no more than an "occasion for writing": what is sought in amphibology is not polysemy, but duplicity. More important still, opposition is never sought for itself, never "honored" as such. When an opposition appears, it is not taken at face value: what one aims at through it is the plurality it implies and not the conflict. As Barthes says regarding Paradox (but this is also true of Antithesis and all antinomic values):

> We do not form oppositions of *named*, fractionized values; we skirt, we avoid, we dodge such values: *we take tangents. (RB,* 140)

The avowed goal of this approach is above all to prevent "a meaning from taking hold," to keep "system" from prevailing over the systematic, frozen structure over the process of structuration; in short, to preclude the text's closing in upon itself or degenerating into "dissertation," "boredom," or *pensum.* What was pure drifting in the interior of words is always in danger of congealing into a sticky Image or a constraining concept. The living metaphor traversing the Essay runs the risk of turning into catachresis, and dynamic repetition the risk of turning into the old worn-out refrain.

At the very heart of every Essay there is a "forced movement" (Deleuze) whose amplitude constantly extends beyond the coupling of the basic heterogeneous series themselves and threatens the harmony or rhythm (the "resonance") that it induced in the "system." This is translated into concrete terms in all the negative figures that traverse the Essay: the exhaustion of language—"He sees language in the figure of an exhausted old woman" (*RB,* 177); death—"I am speaking about myself as if I were more or less dead" (*RB,* 168); the poisoning of meaning, Stupidity; clichés of Image—"I am pigeonholed, assigned to an (intellectual) site" (*RB,* 49), or "Nothing can be done: I have to go through the Image: the Image is a sort of social military service: I cannot have myself exempted from it: I cannot obtain a medical waiver, I cannot desert" (*PRB,* 305). Or even antithesis, antinomy, binarism (*RB,* 138), the temptation of the final word, or the degeneration of discourse into boastfulness, prattling, or fine phrases. Like any discourse, the Essayist's can become repetitive, abstract, worn-out, with its most original utterances deformed into vulgate or into clichés.

As soon as there is a mutation of discourse somewhere, there follows a vulgate and its exhausting cortège of motionless phrases. (*RB*, 53)

Finally, in spite of the renunciation of mastery and the precautions that the Essayist may take in order to thwart the constraints of Meaning and to escape the snares of system, at every instant his discourse threatens to join the "layer" of assertive or "veritative" discourse:

His (sometimes acute) discomfort—mounting some evening . . . to a kind of fear—was generated by his sense of producing a double discourse, whose mode overreached its aim, somehow: for the aim of his discourse is not truth, and yet this discourse is assertive. (*RB*, 48)

It seems that parallel to the differential order of the fragments and "details" that condition the "internal resonance" of the Essay as "system," an "order" of a completely different dimension troubles its economy: an order dominated this time by ideas of "exhaustion," of death, of *Fading*, of repetition or exclusion, an order that, as it were, constantly contests from the inside the play of fragments and allegories that punctuate its fundamental discontinuity. Despite everything, there appears to be a sort of negativity at work in the Essay, "a work of the negative" that seeks to undermine the equilibrium of exchanges between the series and constantly threatens to annul the infinite play of *reflection* that they command in the text. Such at least would be the case if the third "order" that I am considering here reintroduced the classical category of "conflict" and if, in the final analysis, it were a matter of simple displacement or transfer to other terms of the category of *opposition*. But the "forced movement" of great magnitude that overflows the base series in a movement of "diverging" (*déport*) makes all the categories of this type inoperative and obsolete: the "forced movement" is the "procedure" (another) that produces the idea of Neutral and the figures connected to it by integrating them into the system:

"The Neutral is not an average of active and of passive; rather it is a back-and-forth, an amoral oscillation, in short, one might say, the converse of an antinomy. As value (proceeding from the region Passion), the Neutral would correspond to the force by which social praxis sweeps away and renders unreal scholastic antinomies." (*RB*, 132)

In this way, the forced movement that overflows the Essay's basic utterances does not refer to a "negativity"—to an exhaustion of language or to a death—but to a text that is capable of integrating the contradiction, owing to the production of the category Neutral. Since it is not the third term (category Zero) of an unimaginatively semantic or purely conflictual opposition, but "at another link of the infinite chain of language, the second term of a new paradigm, of which violence (combat, victory, theater, arrogance) is the primary term" (*RB*, 132–133), the Neutral gives rise to a "generalized collapse" of the economies of the Text (*S/Z*, 215):

(1) *The economy of language*, "usually protected by the separation of opposites" is fundamentally questioned: the lexicon is twisted in ways that would be impossible elsewhere (exuberant neologisms, *mots-tiroirs*, transliterations, shifts, inventions): syntax is turned around (no more logical cells, no more obligatory transitional sentences; punctuation is thrown out, reinvented: the novel use of the colon, for example, interruption of subordination, parataxis, anacoluthon, asyndeton, and so on.)

(2) *The economy of genres* itself is questioned.[54] By abolishing paradigmatic slash marks, the production of the category Neutral in fact provokes a "catastrophic collapse" from the point of view of a certain economy of knowledge and certain expository modes of thought, but, above all, it assumes the form of an "unrestrained metonymy" that here also destroys "the power of legal substitution on which meaning is based" (*S/Z*, 216). With the neutral, it is "no longer possible to safeguard an order of just equivalence; in a word, it is no longer possible to *represent*" (ibid.), and moreover: along with the necessity to *articulate legally* the different types of utterances, the need to have recourse to the various modalities of presentation and exposition of classical rhetorical composition also disappears. The order of the dictionary or any other order will suffice, provided, however — but this is not obligatory — that this order is not entirely arbitrary:

Of the glossary, I keep only its most formal principle: the order of its units." (*RB*, 148)[55]

When the "arcana of meaning" are subverted, when the "sacred" separation between paradigmatic poles is abolished, when one removes the separating barrier ("*la barre de l'opposition*," as Barthes says) that is the basis of all pertinence, a "catastrophe" occurs: "there is an explosive shock, a paradigmatic conflagration" (*S/Z*, 65), that frees up the canons of a text's rhetorical "presentation" and allows for overstepping the conditions defined by rhetoric for the text's composition.

Thus, the idea of Neutral rips away the figures we have thought to be inalienably associated with a "work of the negative" and refers them back to a fundamental positivity of the fragmental text of the Essay:

Figures of the Neutral: white writing . . . Adamic language —
delectable insignificance — the smooth — the empty, the seamless — the
vacancy of the "person," if not annulled at least rendered
irretrievable — absence of *imago* — the suspension of judgment, of due
process — displacement — the refusal "to keep oneself in countenance"
(the refusal of any countenance whatever) — the principle of delicacy —

drifting—pleasure in its ecstatic aspect: whatever avoids or thwarts or ridicules ostentation, mastery, intimidation. (*RB*, 132)

So many figures (except this "vacancy of the person" to which I shall return), so many genres it would have been impossible to integrate into the same text but that now, thanks to the "power" of the Essay as an intensive system, are able not only to coexist but to collaborate in making the Essay the extraordinary text I seek to define under the category "reflective text": a text in which opposites are abolished at the same time that pseudonatural hierarchies and generic frontiers are transgressed.[56]

A book of learning and of writing, at once a perfect system and the mockery of all systems, a summa of intelligence and of pleasure, a vengeful and tender book, corrosive and pacific, etc. (here, a foam of adjectives, an explosion of the image-repertoire). (RB, 173–174)

Thus, there will no longer be any rhetorical constraint nor any generic exclusiveness: the Essay is this text in which all is grist that comes to its mill, a text of the "mélange of genres." It is only with our recognition of what is at stake, with the modern conception of Text and Subject, of reading and writing, that the Essay now begins to enter *theoretically* the history of Literature.

But if the "forced movement" of great magnitude produces the idea of maximum gap and—by means of drifting and paradigmatic conflagration—goes beyond the notion of conflict, it is this same "movement" that is at the origin of one of the dominant figures of the Barthesian Essay: that which Genette's work has taught us to recognize under the category of *prolepsis*.[57] Since all Mastery is rejected, since the security offered by system and by rhetorical composition is no longer needed, the drifting—the "sliding" (*glissement*), as Barthes puts it—will have to be concretely translated through a perpetual "anticipation" of the work. In other words, unable (unwilling) to content himself with inherent, intrinsic limits with the economy of *one* Genre, the essayist will have to anticipate his work and the Essay will have to be defined as the "provisional commentary" on the work. Of a work that consequently will always be a work to come—the future work—the announcement or advertisement, written in the meantime, of the comprehensive, "summative" book that is still to appear. Or, if you like, of the book that, in not being written, becomes this work itself. As Barthes says in a fragment aptly entitled *Later*:

He has a certain foible of providing "introductions," "sketches," "elements," postponing the "real" book till later. This foible has a rhetorical name: *prolepsis* (well discussed by Genette). . . .
These projects, generally heralding a summative, excessive book, parodic of the great monument of knowledge, can only be simple acts of discourse (prolepses indeed); they belong to the category of the dila-

tory. But the dilatory, denial of reality (of the realizable), is no less alive for all that: these projects live; they are never abandoned; suspended, they can return to life at any moment; or at least, like the persistent trace of an obsession, they fulfill themselves, partially, indirectly, *as gestures*, through themes, fragments, articles. (*RB*, 173)

In this way, no matter what form prolepsis may take in the work — project, dilatory maneuver, Prospectus, Program Compulsion — it figures as a fundamental category of the Essay and enables us to account for the perpetual drifting that defines it: "a staircase that never stops" (*RB*, 175). Therefore, at this level, the Essay is defined not only by the coupling of heterogeneous series that edge it, and by the double resonance it induces in the system at the level of fragments and details, but also by the forced movement from which the dimension of the Neutral and its consequences derive.

10. The Book of the Self: Tactics without Strategy

As I have tried to show, the dimension of the Neutral calls for a wide-ranging reexamination of the economies of the text. Nevertheless, one might think that the upheaval it induces into the system would not undermine one of the categories where reinscription of a minimum of unification and identity had long been attempted: the subject of enunciation. Indeed, even in the most "exploded" texts it had always been thought that a certain unity, despite everything, could be instituted and a certain origin assigned by referring to the category of Author, or to that of Scriptor or "fabricator."[58] Generally, no matter how roundabout the approach and no matter what the concessions made to the Essay's fragmentation and discontinuity, the category of the subject of enunciation, as originary principle of the text's production, always appears at one moment or another. Like the phoenix, the author is always reborn from his ashes.[59] But this is not the case in the Essay: to believe that the category of subject as simple origin of the work remains intact after the economy of the text has been so profoundly overturned is to fall victim to an old opposition.

One could not transgress the "wall" of Meaning and the frontier of Genres and expect the category of Subject to remain intact:

An American . . . student identifies, as if it were self-evident, *subjectivity* and *narcissism*; no doubt he thinks that subjectivity consists in talking about oneself, and in speaking well of oneself. This is because he is a victim of the old couple, the old paradigm: *subjectivity/ objectivity*. Yet today the subject apprehends himself *elsewhere*, and "subjectivity" can return at another place on the spiral: deconstructed, taken apart, shifted, without anchorage: why should I not speak of "myself" since this "my" is no longer "the self"? (*RB*, 168)

In producing the dimension of the Neutral in the Essay, the "forced movement" not only induces a "paradigmatic conflagration" that overturns the logico-philosophic economy of Meaning and the rhetorical economy of literary Genres, but also renders the classical category of Subject (Author, Scriptor, Genius, etc.) completely inoperative. Here also, a reversal or more exactly a "deporting" (*déport*) takes place: at the origin of the work (even if it is "exploded") is no longer Subject, identified and identical to itself, but the formal structure of the work which at each of its levels produces subjects: like "passive" Selves correlative to these resonances, these folds, these fires of language, these miraculous encounters among words, making it seem that the subject is snatched up by the text. Like "embryonic subjects" of dynamisms that traverse the text each time one code is "set aslant" by another, each time a known language is unexpectantly crossed by a language (by nature) foreign to it, each time the law of one Genre is transgressed in a carnivalesque mode. But also each time an embryo of story sees itself relayed by another, each time an utterance begun on a given pronominal register *is completed* on another. It is this "sliding" (*glissement*), this utterly extraordinary production of multiple and heterogeneous "subjects," this proliferation of sites and subjects of enunciation (and therefore, of reception) that is "recounted" in the fragment Barthes devotes to *Personal Pronouns* where, as he says, "everything happens":

> The so-called personal pronouns: everything happens here, I am forever enclosed within the pronominal lists: "I" mobilizes the image-repertoire, "you" and "he" mobilize paranoia. But, also, fugitively, according to the reader, everything, like the reflections of a watered silk, can be reversed: in "myself, I," the "I" might not be "me," the "me" he so ostentatiously puts down; I can say to myself "you" as Sade did, in order to detach within myself the worker, the fabricator, the producer of writing, from the subject of the work (the Author); on the other hand, not to speak of oneself can mean: *I am He who does not speak about himself*; and to speak about oneself by saying "he" can mean: *I am speaking about myself as though I were more or less dead*, caught up in a faint mist of paranoiac rhetoric, or again: I am speaking about myself in the manner of the Brechtian actor who must distance his character, etc.
> (*RB*, 168)

The Barthesian Essay is thus defined not only by the resonance of coupled series, not only by the forced movement that induces "deportings," displacements, ruptures in tone and in genre, but also by an *entire colony of subjects*: paranoiac and mad subjects, passive subjects prey to the Imaginary, workers, manufacturers, producers of writing. A series of deaths and resurrections fills the smallest interstices of the text and they are just so many "subjects" of the work, like the Author. Therefore, beside the resonance from which proceeds the highly original unity of the Barthesian Essay, beside the forced movement that enables us to account for the dynamisms traversing the text, there is an essential *third dimension* in the Essay: that dimension which now enables us to account for the proliferation of the "centers" of enunciation and for their fundamental heterogeneity: that dimension which also enables us to understand that a text need not be the product of a unified or unique source in order to have a real unity: here it is no longer the Author who produces a Work, but rather the *formal structure* of the text—the protocols of production and enunciation (procedures) molded by it—that produces at once the utterances and the subjects that will serve as their supports. But it should be noted here that the same movement, the same dynamics, and the same "shock" bring about both this calling into question, this pluralization, this dissemination of the subject, and the remodeling of the economy of Genres:

> The intrusion, into the discourse of the essay, of a third person who nonetheless refers to no fictive creature marks the necessity of remodeling the genres: let the essay avow itself *almost* a novel: a novel without proper names." (*RB*, 120)

The Essay (for Montaigne and Barthes and Valéry, for example) as "book of the self" or "self-portrait" can thus be understood neither as the instrument for the expression of an Author's "ideas," nor as the "self-presence" of a Self[60] that is identical to itself from one end of the text to the other; it must be seen as a "resistance" to a "spontaneous" movement that can only be the repetition of outworn ideas, the refurbishing of already familiar sites, the culling of "stock phrases" and "images":

> This book is not the book of his ideas; it is the book of the Self, the book of my resistances to my own ideas; it is a *recessive* book (which falls back, but which may also gain perspective thereby). (*RB*, 119)

In this sense, like every "modern" work, the Essay does not raise problems of meaning, but rather a *problem of usage* (Deleuze) or, in other words, a problem of *effect and of functioning*.

> The book does not choose, it functions by alternation, it proceeds by impulses of the image-system pure and simple and by critical approaches, but these approaches are never anything but effects of resonance: nothing is more a matter of the image-system, of the imaginary, than (self-)criticism." (*RB*, 120)

The essayist is *acutely aware of his debt to Rhetoric.* In fact, it is this consciousness of the insistent and silent presence of *Commonplaces*, of the unpliable character of the *Encyclopedia*, of the Stock Phrases and Images used by rhetorical

Mnemotechnics that determines the plethora of formal inventions and the frenzy with which the essayist ceaselessly contributes to the skirting of the "wall" that all these rhetorical figures oppose to every innovation, every attempt to break with what has *already* been said, *already* formulated.[61] This may perhaps explain that "rage" so frequent among essayists—their impassioned attempts to skirt this wall, whether it be called Nature, Stereotype, Meaning, System, Dissertation, Plan, or Composition. Perhaps it is also for this reason that there are always at least two stages in the development of the smallest utterance: a first stage in which one conforms to the rule of language and the world as *Physis* (whether of a rhetorical or a philosophical order); and a second stage, the reprise, in which one displaces (contests) through a movement of re-writing what has been uttered "from time immemorial." It will not be surprising to discover that this "second" movement or as Barthes says, this "mania of the second degree" (*RB*, 66) finds its basis in the dimension of the Neutral:

> No Nature. In a first period, everything comes down to the struggle between a *pseudo-Physis* (*Doxa*, the natural, etc.) and an *anti-Physis* (all my personal utopias): one is to be hated, the other to be desired. Yet, in some later period, this very struggle seems theatrical to him; it is then, surreptitiously, repulsed, distanced by the defense (the desire) of the Neutral. (*RB*, 132)

It is this third dimension that enables us to account for one of the most interesting and least remarked characteristics of the Essay (Montaignian or Barthesian): having renounced the economy of philosophic system that commands the idea of Mastery, having in the same movement dismissed the economy of literary Genres insofar as it commands the ordered exchange of different modes of enunciation (Discourse or Narrative in particular), the Essay appears as one of those rare literary texts in which literariness asserts itself from beginning to end: as a *tactics without strategy*:

> The movement of his work is tactical: a matter of displacing himself, of obstructing, as with bars, but not of conquering. . . . This work would therefore be defined as: *a tactics without strategy*. (*RB*, 172)

Along with the outlines, the dissertations on set topics, and the rules of composition, the whole scene of language as *Topos of Battle* and terrain of *Conflict*—the doxological and ideological space of thought as *Kampfplatz* (Kant)—is "superseded" in a "deporting movement." Indeed, what leads us to think of and experience the Essay as a "reflective text" is the possibility of a plural text with multiple networks that "interact without any of them being able to surpass the rest" (*S/Z*, 5): an "ideal" text whose way was prepared in *S/Z* on the basis of a reading of a short story by Balzac and that *Roland Barthes by Roland Barthes, The Pleasure of the Text*, and *A Lover's Discourse* put directly into practice in developing its theory. A text that is no longer the assumption of an ultimate signified, but a "galaxy of signifiers": "it has no beginning; it is reversible, we gain access to it by several entrances, none of which can be authoritatively declared to be the main one" (*S/Z*, 5).

At least one question remains: to whom is a text of this nature addressed? What becomes of its reader?

11. A New Reading Space

No "thesis" on the pleasure of the text is possible; barely an inspection (an introspection) that falls short. *Eppure si gaude!* And yet, against and in spite of everything, the text gives me bliss. (*PT*, 34)

Contrary to appearances, the different definitions of the Essay we have encountered are not contradictory. "Tactics without strategy," the Essay is essentially (though not exclusively) opposed to the philosophical system and the economy of Learning and Subject it commands.

"A novel without proper names," the Essay is opposed rather to rhetorical rule and, in particular, to the economy of the classical ("readerly") Text and to the division of Genres. But, generally, it is always the coherence and unicity of the Subject of enunciation as the unique principle of the production and organization of the Text that are signalled and denounced as illusions.[62]

In an Essay, the subject of enunciation is always a *partial effect* of the overall functioning of the text. When the identity and unicity of the subject of enunciation (the Author) of the essayistic text are fortuitous and fragmentary—"subjects" other than the Author people the Essay—the identity and the unicity of the *reader himself* are undermined as well. Far from relying for its reading and the apprehension of its Unity on *one* reader, unified and identical to himself, the Essay is this text that destroys the last category that was to provide a resolution of the problem of the Unity so peculiar to the fragmental work in general and to the Essay in particular: the Reader. As "a tactics without strategy," or as "a novel without proper names," the Essay can therefore be defined now as a text that is based less on the psychology or thought of *one* Author than on a "theory" of the different "postures" assumed in a necessarily *desultory* and circular manner by the presumed Author of the text as well as by the Reader: the one inasmuch as her writing is always already a practice of reading (a lexeo*graphy*); the other inasmuch as her reading is always a certain way of writing or re-writing the text (a sub-*scription*). It is this rotation of "roles" and these displacements that Barthes, with his usual vigilance, describes in the fragment entitled *I see language*:

According to an initial vision, the image-repertoire [*l'imaginaire*] is simple: it is the discourse of others *insofar as I see it* (I put it between quotation marks). Then I turn the scopia on myself: I see my language *in so far as it is seen*: I see it *naked* (without quotation marks): this is the disgraced, pained phase of the image-repertoire. A third vision then appears: that of infinitely spread-out languages, of parentheses never to be closed: a utopian vision in that it supposes a mobile, plural reader, who nimbly inserts and removes the quotation marks: who begins to write *with me*. (*RB*, 161)

In this way, from the *formal point of view* of the work, the traditional hierarchy that separates the Author of a work from its Reader — this kind of precedence of the former over the latter — is obsolete in the Essay: neither surpasses the other, neither can be considered the unique "donor" or the ultimate organizer (*ordonnateur*) of the work. Just as there is (was) no *first* reading for the writing of the text and the production of its utterances, so there is no *final* reading: the author is no more the "master" of what he wrote than the reader is the slave of what he reads.[63]

The only difference here is that contrary to the "readerly" text, the Essay is itself a text that is already discontinuous. Just as the Author's identity is a fortuitous one — since in the final instance it rests on a "secret system of phantasms" unknown even to the author — so the reader's identity and unicity are extrinsic and accidental. However deeply he explores the various degrees and levels of an Essay's discourse, it will always be the figures in which he recognizes himself that he comes up against, and the signifiers with which he is particularly taken that he will identify as the "subject" of the text. That is why, in a certain way, no "thesis" whatsoever on the Meaning or Origin of an Essay is possible: "Barely an inspection (an introspection) that *falls short*."

In other words, the general economy that ruled over the "consumption" of the "classical" text is subverted: the Author is *at once* a producer and a product of his work; and the reader is no longer a passive consumer. She must also compose the work in her own way, decipher it as one deciphers a musical score or a palimpsest. Thus, reading is no longer consumption, "but play (that play which is the return of the different)" (*S/Z*, 16).

These two edges of the text (writing/reading) refer to the "matricial" or "machinic" aspect of the mode of functioning of the Essay; in fact, from the point of view of its production, it essentially refers to a "theory" of "subjects" irreducible to each other in which the Author appears as a *produced figure* (one of the "subjects"); from the point of view of its reading, it refers to a *multiplicity of possible readers* that defines a *new reading space* of the text: open and not hierarchized.[64] Based on a "going-beyond" of the metaphysical category of Author, essayistic writing presupposes a true *Typology of readers* corresponding to the displacements it carries out at the level of the different modes of enunciation (I/You/Me) and at the different levels of the structuration of the text:

We can imagine a typology of the pleasures of reading – or of the readers of pleasure. . . . The fetishist would be matched up with the divided-up text, the singling out of quotations, formulae, turns of phrase, with the pleasure of the word. The obsessive would experience the voluptuous release of the letter, of secondary, disconnected languages, of metalanguages (this class would include all the logophiles, linguists, semioticians, philologists: all those for whom language *returns*). A paranoiac would consume or produce complicated texts, stories developed like arguments, constructions posited like games, like secret constraints. As for the hysteric (so contrary to the obsessive), he would be the one who takes the text *for ready money*, who joins in the bottomless, truthless comedy of language, who is no longer the subject of any critical scrutiny and *throws himself* across the text (which is quite different from projecting himself into it). (*PT*, 63)

Through these different types of readers, it is easy to recognize, but this time named and indexed on the basis of the grid of analytic discourse (there are other possible grids), the "theory" of ideal "subjects" brought into play by the Essay's formal structure. Parallel to the multiplicity of "embryonic subjects" and "passive Selves" that populate the Essay, a series of readers comes to occupy the "new space" of writing and reading that the Essay defines: "Unimaginable space, escaping any constraints of optics, escaping any consideration of the whole, essentially nonfinite, disunited, discontinuous" (Maurice Blanchot, *L'Entretien infini*, 413–414).

When Barthes writes that he would like to have produced "not a comedy of the Intellect but its *romanesque*" (*RB*, 90), we have every reason at present to think that he had in mind a very special text – the Essay: a plural and mobile text where the dissolution of the categories of Author and Reader no longer implies the "explosion" of the work or cacophony, but on the contrary, the multiplication of words and perspectives, the broadening of points of view and the affirmation of a "fragmentary experience" of language (Blanchot) opening on another mode of completion of the text: "Hence the ideal would be: neither a text of vanity, nor a text of lucidity, but a text with uncertain quotation marks, with floating parentheses (never to close the parenthesis is very specifically: *to drift*). This also depends on the reader, who produces the *spacing* of the readings" (*RB*, 106).

12. The Essay: A "Consideration of Effects"

Together with the rejection of the constraints of the philosophical system, renouncing the economy of the Subject automatically entails a reconsideration of the classical category of "thought." When the essayist's discourse ceases to rest on the prior identity and cohesion of a Subject or on the unicity of a Principle, the category of "thought" itself is, in turn, questioned and subverted: the Essay no longer presents itself as a homogeneous text that "expounds" a "thought," but as a "literary machine" intended to produce effects, or as Barthes puts it, a "consideration of effects."[65]

This last definition of the Essay enables us to understand what might be the finality of a text that openly avows having no strategic goal and constituting only one *tactic*: in fact, not based on any "instance of truth," the Essay reflects a double movement. As a "tactics without strategy," the Essay essentially designated, as we have seen, a certain mode of utilization and transfiguration of the "objects of knowledge and dissertation," a certain way of arranging the apparently most heteroclitic contents without totalization. This first movement characterizes the *mode of production* of the Essay's utterances and relates to the procedures enabling it to produce its particular Unity. But as a "consideration of effects," the Essay relates to a "new intellectual art" (*RB*, 90) that consists less in expounding once and for all a system of thoughts than in playing in a festive manner, in miming or simulating all the "postures" and all the "figures" that a given theme (Writing, the Text, Pleasure, or Love, for example) can arouse in *any potential reader*: the essential being that "it work" and that here and there, discontinuously but surely, the reader be "taken in." This second movement—inseparable from the first—thus characterizes the *mode of possible reception* of the Essay and relates to the type of *efficacy* it seeks. A "tactics without strategy," the Essay refers to what is literally "intractable" in a given theme: namely what is irreducible to a unique philosophical principle or to an identity. As a "consideration of effects," a "reflective text," it relates to the "machinic" (structural) aspect of the text: "It offers the reader a discursive site" (*LDF*, 3), as Barthes says, in a generalized system of exchanges among the most diverse languages. But being *the one and the other* at the same time, it becomes *simulation*:

> Everything follows from this principle: that the lover is not to be reduced to a simple symptomal subject, but rather that we hear in his voice what is "unreal," i.e., intractable. Whence the choice of a "dramatic" method which renounces examples and rests on the single action of a primary language (no metalanguage). The description of the lover's discourse has been replaced by its simulation, and to that discourse has been restored its fundamental person, the *I*, in order to stage an utterance, not an analysis. (*LDF*, 3)

I shall return shortly to the need to "dramatize" the method and to the "theatre" to which it refers. Note here the relationship between this "simulation" and what Sade brought into play in the *120 Days* when he wrote: "If we had not said everything, analyzed everything, how could we have guessed what suits you? *It is up to you to take and to leave the rest*; another will do as much, and, little by little, *everything will find its place*."

The exhaustive enumeration of scriptural or lectural positions, the circulation of all types of "subjects" inhabiting or traversing the Barthesian Essay, but above all, the great profusion of details, allegories, scenes, and miniature tableaux constituting the text have no other purpose: it is a matter, here and there and through chance encounters, of making the reader recognize (herself in) a "scene of language," and take an active part in the text that she reads. On every page, the essayist seems to be telling the reader: among all the figures the text offers you here, it is up to you to pick and choose, and to leave the rest:

> Figures take shape insofar as we can recognize, in passing discourse, something that has been read, heard, felt. The figure is outlined (like a sign) and memorable (like an image or a tale). A figure is established if at least someone can say: *That's so true! I recognize that scene of language. (LDF*, 4)

Like the Sadian "tableau"—well analyzed by Barthes himself—the Barthesian "detail" or "allegory" is on the order of the Lacanian "signifier": like it, they "represent," in Lacan's terms, "the subject for another signifier."[66] In the Essay (for Barthes and for Montaigne as well) the "detail," the "scene," the "right" word and, in a general way, all the "fires of language," all the "lucky finds" that traverse it, give rise to a double movement: on the one hand, as "sensual objects" that seem to spring out of the text, they literally *impose* themselves on the reader: "I do not resist!" Barthes writes. "Their form has taken me in!" On the other hand, and inversely, the reader, losing his place as a passive consumer, at one moment or another should soon feel implicated ("taken up") by such and such a "scene," ravished (in every sense of the term) by such and such a "detail." Recognizing a certain "scene of language," I recognize *myself*. This was everything the essayist needed! Such, in any case, are the "tactics" and the "thought" for which he aimed.

One must, here too (Tort, "L'Effet-Sade," 74), want at any cost to "recover" Barthes (or Montaigne, or Leiris, or Blanchot), "to exalt them naively" (narcissistically) or to deny the specificity of their work in order to pass over in silence the completely "special" function played by the "details" the "allegories," and, in short, by all the "sensual objects" that densely populate the essayistic text and condition its mode of "composition" and "unity." It is at their level that the changes we find in going from one Essay to another—namely, the *style* and general *tonality* of the work—have their foundation. And it is for this essential reason that the type of effect produced by an Essay is absolutely indissociable from the name of its *composer*: thus, renaming the concept Michel Tort meant to characterize the specific efficacy of the Sadian work, I propose naming this decisive function of the Barthesian Essay: the *Barthes-effect*.

13. Reflection Generalized

The question has been raised here several times: What makes for the unity of the Essay? How is it that, in spite of the great disparity in the utterances and genres it brings into play, we nonetheless have a genuine sense of its unity and take pleasure in the text? At the outset of this study, I found it necessary to begin by giving up the search for this unity in a principle that would unify all the parts, a prior Whole that would assemble the fragments. It then appeared that the One and the All that I sought was not the product of a unique principle but the effect of an "internal resonance" in a generalized system of exchanges between disconnected parts. But what can be seen clearly now is that this "effect" is neither an illusion nor an extrinsic and secondary function of the Essay. It is an absolutely central dimension:

> Speaking of a text, he credits its author with not manipulating the reader. But he found this compliment by discovering that he himself does all he can to manipulate the reader, and that in fact he will never renounce an art of *effects*. (*RB*, 102)

Elsewhere, Barthes gives this crucial explanation:

> He wants to side with any writing whose principle is that *the subject is merely an effect of language*. He imagines an enormous science, in the utterance of which the scientist would at last include himself—the science of the effects of language. (*RB*, 79)

Called sometimes "Bathmology" (science of "the degrees of language" [*RB*, 67]) and sometimes "Hyphology" (science of the text as a "spider's web" where the subject "unmakes himself" and dissolves himself [*PT*, 64]), this "science" is not a myth: it refers to a theory and to a practice of the text whose principle is precisely that "the subject is merely an effect of language." Through the constant implication of the "subject" of writing *and* of the reading it involves, the Barthesian essay thus rests, in the final analysis, on the efficacy of *a system of signal-signs*—a "signaletics," says Barthes—that conditions the type of specific effects it produces. Contrary to the concept or the idea, the "sensual object" is thus defined as "phantasm" or "simulacrum" (signal-sign) and the Essay as *simulation* or *theater*, the effect of the functioning of "detail," of the "scene of language," or of "allegory" as "literary machine":

> At the crossroads of the entire *oeuvre*, perhaps the Theater: there is not a single one of his texts, in fact, which fails to deal with a certain theater, and spectacle is the universal category in whose aspect the world is seen. . . . What has attracted him is less the sign than the signal, the poster: the science he desired was not a semiology but a *signaletics*. (*RB*, 177)

Signaletics as theatrical simulation designates, above all, the power to produce an *effect*. No longer in the causal sense, however, but in the sense of a "sign" "stemming from a process of signalization; and it is in the sense of 'costume' or rather mask, expressing a process of disguise where, behind every mask, there is still another . . ." (Deleuze, *Logique du sens*, 304): is it by chance, then, that Barthes writes the following with respect to his *Roland Barthes*:

> All this must be considered as if spoken by a character in a novel—or rather by several characters. For the image-repertoire [l'imaginaire], fatal substance of the novel, and the labyrinth of levels in which anyone who speaks about himself gets lost—the image-repertoire is taken over by several masks (*personae*), distributed according to the depth of the stage (and yet no one—*personne*, as we say in French—is behind them). (*RB*, 119–120)

A non-hierarchized and non-centered work, since it "functions by alternation" (ibid.) and constantly reflects a discontinuous reading, the essay is therefore defined as a "digest of coexistence" or, if you prefer, a "set of simultaneous events" (Deleuze, op. cit., 303) where the categories of Author, Reader, and Critic can exchange their "role" in a superimposition of figures in which each one will at one moment or another find its place. But the "false pretender" can no longer be called "false" in relation to any instance of truth, any more than simulation can be called an appearance or an illusion.

The Barthes-effect—and what could be called the reflecting-effect as a fourth dimension of the essayistic text in general—is this power of simulation. It is the phantasm itself, that is, the effect of the functioning of the simulacrum as *textual machine*.[67]

This aspect of the matter can be put in the form of a basic axiom: The Essay is a text in which the arrangement of details, figures, scenes of language, etc., is so organized that *for every reader* there is at least one figure that cleaves him (Tort, "L'Effet-Sade," 75). The essential thing is no longer expressing a thought or telling a story, but seeing to it that at the end of the book "everything will have found its place," that is to say that the reader, whatever his "tastes," will have found his place in one or another of the figures offered him.

Here, again, we have to do with a principle of textual functioning of the same type as that found in Sade's work: "Certainly, many of the indiscretions (*écarts*) which you will see portrayed will displease you, we know that, but there will be others that will warm you to the point of titillation, and this is what we seek." The reader for pleasure, the essayist, or the amorous subject basically say nothing else: among the many figures presented to you, there is sure to be one that will please and gratify you, and that is all we need: "Another will do the same, and little by little everything will have found its place."

This final aspect of my investigation will perhaps show why I have re-inscribed the essay as a *reflective* text: in the essay, it is not only a matter of enabling the reader at any moment to *recognize* himself in one or another of the figures presented to him, but *at the same time*, a matter of repeating, miming, or simulating what has yet to be accomplished: projects, programs.

This can explain, moreover, the many dilatory maneuvers that run through the text, all its programmatic compulsions and the proposals it offers for consideration: in every instance, it is a question of running through all the "fringes of the spectrum," of covering the maximum range of possibilities, so that the most exacting reader can ultimately say: "I recognize this scene of language." Thus, like the fantasy dictation of which Barthes writes in *Sade/Fourier/Loyola*, the essayistic text is *dictation* (*dictée*) or *dictator*:

> The image ["detail"] appears to originate a program, the program a text, and the text a practice; however, this practice is itself written; it returns (for the reader) to program, to text, to fantasy: nothing remains but an inscription with a multiple tense: fantasy *announces* memory; writing is not anamnesis but catamnesis." (*SFL*, 164)

It is this catamnesis that perhaps best characterizes the reflective effect of the essayistic text as the inscription, in the very body (*corps*) of the text, of a plural body (*corps*) where the most diverse kinds of readers can find themselves. This catamnesis defines the Essay, or rather the reader(s) of an Essay, as a veritable "Society of Friends of the Text," whose members

> would have nothing in common (for there is no necessary agreement on the texts of pleasure), but their enemies . . . Such a society would have no site, could function only in total atopia; yet it would be a kind of phalanstery, for in it contradictions would be acknowledged (and the risks of ideological imposture thereby restricted), difference would be observed, and conflict rendered insignificant (being unproductive of pleasure). (*PT*, 14–15)

14. Oh, a Friend!

It is evident that the object of all his work is a morality of the sign (*morality* is not *morale*). (*RB*, 97)

In Montaigne's *Essays*, the central character of the first book was a blind spot: the lost friend La Boétie. In the second book, it is Montaigne himself who comes to the forefront. But the third book enables Montaigne to discover a friend, a *virtual* reader—an "ideal" reader—for whom the work is waiting and for whom it has, as it were, prepared a place:

> If by such good signs I knew of a man who was suited to me, truly I would go very far to find him; for the sweetness of harmonious and agreeable company cannot be bought too dearly, in my opinion. Oh, a friend! (III. 9, 750)

But Montaigne writes this with the secret knowledge that he can only fantasize this "friend," this being who would be "suitable" to him, as he puts it, he can only inscribe him in his work as an emptiness and wait. This helps to explain the sententious remark that follows his "appeal," where he speaks somewhat sadly of La Boétie:

> I know well that I will leave behind no sponsor anywhere near as affectionate and understanding about me as I was about him. There is no one to whom I would be willing to entrust myself fully for a portrait; he alone enjoyed my true image, and carried it away. That is why I myself decipher myself so painstakingly. (III. 9, 752)

We know (cf. Butor, *Essais sur les Essais*, 215) that Montaigne will eventually delete this last passage in the Bordeaux copy: O Miracle, in the meantime his appeal has been heard by Mlle. de Gournay. Other friends, other readers will later come to "join" Montaigne and form a "Society of Friends of Montaigne." But what Montaigne perhaps could not suspect is that his "humors," as he calls them, have continued to please and be compatible with more "friends" than any author could possibly know during his lifetime. But this is because the field of "friendship" to which the essayistic text as text of pleasure refers is less a question of a psychology of readers than of a typology which itself rests on a *topic*:

> The effort must be made to speak of friendship as of a pure *topic*: this releases me from the field of affectivity — which could not be spoken *without embarrassment*, since it belongs to the order of the imaginary (or rather: I can tell from my embarrassment that the imaginary is very close at hand: I am getting warm). (*RB*, 65)

The original image, the "true image" being always already that which I give to the one I "would like to be" (*RB*, 99) here also implies going beyond the category of author for the benefit of a multiplication of "traits" and "details" that both Author and Reader (his "friend") share according to the fluctuations of their "humors."

Friendship

Contrary to appearances, this beloved "theme" has not always had the same meaning in Barthes's work. For essential reasons, Barthes subjected this theme to a kind of "migration" of meaning that "transported" it from the "worldly" sphere — that of close "friends" in a seminar or the editorial committee of a journal or publishing firm — to a sphere where, as we shall see, "friendship" becomes the motif of a reflection that, paradoxically, focuses less on what friendship is supposed to bring to shared experience, than on how it alienates me, distances me from myself and makes me defer, as it were, the moment of taking care of myself. Faithful to his wily dialectics, Barthes — *altogether consciously*, as we shall see — submits the theme, apparently the least liable to "duplicity" or ambiguity, to the logic of the "swivel" and the spiral: a positive and "active" theme, it gradually receives its "reactive" counterpoint: indispensable, "friendship" nevertheless remains marked by connotations that sway it toward negative values.

To what can this ambivalence be attributed? And is it simply a matter of "ambivalence?" We cannot answer these questions—crucial to the understanding of the "later" Barthes, and in particular, to the implementation of an "ethical" reflection that becomes increasingly insistent in the latter works—without at least roughly sketching out the component elements of this "motif."

Without pretending to examine in detail the history of this theme, it seems that in the '70s the term began to take on the "turn" it would later exhibit in works such as *The Pleasure of the Text*, *A Lover's Discourse*, or *Roland Barthes by Roland Barthes*. An inattentive reading of the texts in question might easily lead us to think that this is a frequent theme, one dear to the author, that from one occurrence to the next maintains a certain homogeneity—even, indeed, an open "transparency": in short, friendship is Acolouthia, namely, a space where I can escape *Images* and where I can move around without having to justify at every turn the words I use, the tastes I have, the values I privilege, and the like. In other words, friendship is the very opposite of a "neutral" space in the everyday sense of the term: that which Barthes, in an "aristocratic" gesture—whose intertextual "origin," in my opinion, has not been sufficiently explored—refers to or associates with the masses, with the public, or, in Platonic terms, the "great beast." But let us start with Barthes's definition of *Acolouthia*:

> *Acolouthia*: going-beyond (*dépassement*) of contradiction (I interpret: *the release from the snare*). But *Acolouthia* has another sense: the *cortege* of friends who accompany me, guide me, *to whom I yield myself*. By this word, I would like to designate this rare field where ideas penetrate affectivity, where friends, through the cortege by which they accompany your life, enable you to think, write, speak. (*PRB*, 308, emphasis mine)

Kierkegaard, whom Barthes liked to invoke in the works I am considering here, said that it is better to write a work and be able to "retract" it afterwards than to write nothing and therefore have nothing to retract. It is the movement of what Kierkegaard mischievously termed palinode that I shall trace here: addressing a public that is present only to speak about his work and to pay him "friendly" homage, Barthes, in a certain way, *can only* do the same for them. Moreover, he has even less difficulty doing so since his audience is by and large composed of "friends" and close acquaintances (of his work or of himself). But in reading the text closely, one cannot fail to see, inscribed as an emptiness (*en creux*), a movement of "retreat"—completely discreet, it is true, but no less significant in this context—that totally reverses the first perspective: when it is a matter of "friends," *Acolouthia* represents a sort of removal of the "snare" of Images, but despite everything it remains profoundly marked by a negative valence: it still represents a "snare" since I have *to yield myself* (to them), which, in Barthesian terms, means that I have to renounce that which is most authentic in me, most irreducible. The manner in which Barthes is then literally incorporated into the circle of friends, but above all the detour through the Socratic reference in its indication of a veritable movement of denial demonstrates that the "question" of friendship is not at all as clear as might have been imagined originally: that, in any case, it cannot be resolved by a purely "psychological" or "mundane" explanation:

> These friends: I think *for them*, they think *in my head*. In this color of intellectual work (or writing) there is something Socratic: Socrates lectured on the idea, but his method, the step-by-step discourse, was amorous: in order to speak, he needed *the guarantee of inspired love*, the consent of a loved one whose responses marked the progression of reasoning. Socrates knew *Acolouthia*—but (*here I must resist*) he maintained the snare of contradictions in it, the arrogance of truth (nothing surprising in his "sublimation"—refusing Alcibiades *in order to finish*). (*PRB*, 308, emphasis mine)

Thus does Barthes retract *in extremis*. As we shall see, it would be extravagant to "psychologize" the problem too quickly: after all, Barthes, not long before making these remarks at the Colloquium at Cerisy, published his *Roland Barthes*, in which he derides any attempt to submit the text to the psychoanalytical "gendarme." To risk "psychoanalyzing" the movement that makes him withdraw from the game—take his marbles and go home—by having recourse to Socrates would be the best way to fall into the net of the spiderweb that Barthes has so well described for himself and the reader of the text in general: that of our imaginary. Wasn't it Barthes himself who wrote concerning the *Roland Barthes*, a book that exposed him directly to view: "The vital effort of this book is to bring onto the stage before you an image-repertoire" [*imaginaire*] (*RB*, 105)? But it is clear that the imaginary he alluded to here was first of all that which he shared with every possible reader. What do we do then with what we persist in reading as the indication of a real problem? Do we have to attribute it to our own imaginary? I have already shown why such a problematic would no longer be acceptable with regard to the essayistic text as reinvented by Barthes: it is by nature made to provoke in you that which is most regressive, at the same time that it liberates experiences in you that no other type of writing or text can offer. To want to track down *one* imaginary in a text is inevitably to let oneself be somehow taken in. Barthes dreamt of something he called Hyphology, a science of the text as web (*hyphos*): he should have specified that this was a web of the sort the spider weaves using a substance from its own body that has an adhesive or sticky quality. We have been warned: however far we might seek to explore the meanderings of the Barthesian text, there will always be a figure in which our desire to interpret leads us into an abyss!

There is, however, another path (apart from those taken by the political or psychoanalytic "gendarmes"), a path that, with Barthes, I shall call the "privileged relationship":[68] it would not aim at exclusivity of interpretation; nor would it try to lead to something definitive: it would somewhat resemble the method Barthes himself proposed for a new kind of teaching:

> The primary advantage would be to suspend, or at least delay speech roles: so that in listening, speaking, or answering, I should never be the agent of a judgment, constraint, or intimidation, the prosecutor of a case. Certainly calm speech will in the end secrete its own role, since, no matter what I say, the other always reads me as an image; but in the time I would take to elude this role, in the work of language which the community will accomplish . . . a certain depropriation of speech (close thenceforth to writing) will be attained, or even: *a certain generalization of the subject.* (Barthes in *Tel Quel* 47, Autumn 1971, 17–18)

Once more, recapitulation is needed. When Barthes was asked in 1971 about the role that Journals play in his work of "writing," it was quite natural for him to refer to the privileged relationship thus maintained with his friends:

> When writing a text for a journal, one is not thinking of the public so much as of the journal's editorial board; they have the merit of constituting a kind of collective audience, but not, strictly speaking, a public one: it is like the situation in a "studio," in a workshop, or in a "class" (as we speak of the violin class at the Conservatory): one writes for "the class."

But interestingly, Barthes hastens to add:

> The journal — apart from tactical considerations of combat, of solidarity, of which I am not speaking here — the journal is a *stage of writing: the stage where one writes in order to be loved* by all those whom one knows, the prudent, reasonable *stage,* where one *begins* to loosen, without yet breaking, the transferential umbilical cord of language (this stage *is never completely liquidated*: if I didn't have friends, if I didn't have to write for them, would I still have the will to write?). One always comes back to the journal. (*Tel Quel* 47, 95, emphasis mine)

As may be seen, friendship — friends — already determine(s) an essential movement in Barthesian writing: without friendship, he would not even have, or perhaps would no longer have, the mere "courage" to write: one writes "in order to be loved" but also for those one loves. This aspect of things is clearly established here. But it is striking to note that here, too, a certain form of palinode is at work:

after all, this "transferential" movement—the word is Barthes's!—still quasi-Oedipal, only represents one "stage" (the word recurs symptomatically at least three times in the remarks): one day the umbilical "cord" must be cut, children's games put aside, and the act of writing begun: for whom? For oneself? For a larger audience? For one's mother? For no one? As often, with Barthes, it seems at first glance that positive responses to all these questions are plausible. But already a movement of distancing—conceived in an initial stage as a sort of retreat in relation to his own imaginary—is clearly inscribed in the text. In having recourse to the notion of Topic, which will systematically appear whenever friends are concerned, Barthes believes (?) he has found a way out: related to a "field" or to an atopic space, figures and bodies *circulate* without imposing Images on me.[69]

In this sense, *Roland Barthes by Roland Barthes* can be read at first as an attempt to unravel this question: a question that, by implying the problem (of particularity) of the "subject," will be marked with a new "valence," with a new theoretical-philosophical preoccupation in Barthes's works: specifically that which will persist in associating the "field" or "network" constituted by friends with "morality." Or in other words, that which makes friendship the ethical-political problem par excellence.[70] One text (among others) aptly notes this in the *Roland Barthes* and it would be naive to think that it is by chance entitled "Friends":

Friends

He is looking for a definition of the term "morality," which he has read in Nietzsche (the morality of the body among the ancient Greeks), and which he puts in opposition to morals; but he cannot conceptualize it; he can merely attribute to it a kind of training ground, a *topic*. This ground is from all accounts that of friendship [*amitié*], or rather (for this Latinate word is too stuffy, too prudish): of friends [*amis*] (speaking of them, I can never do anything but catch myself up—catch them up—in a contingency—a difference). In this space of *cultivated* affects, he finds the practice of this new subject whose theory is to be sought for today: the friends form a network among themselves and each must be apprehended there as *external/internal*, subjected by each conversation to the question of heterotopia: where am I among my desires? Where am I in relation to desire? The question is put to me by the development of a thousand vicissitudes of friendship. Hence is written, day by day, an ardent text, a magical text, which will never come to an end, a glittering image of the Liberated Book. (*RB*, 64)

It is precisely when the affective disposition put into play by the amical relationship is evoked that Barthes "glides" or, if you prefer, "displaces" the question: not in avoiding it, but rather by "translating" it in such a way that, while continuing to present apparently the "same" traits, the amical relationship carries, in fact, as Montaigne would say, "outside of [his] subject, the seeds of a richer and bolder material." Indeed, if "affectivity" is transformed into a space of *cultivated affects*—which, it is understood, is not at all the same thing!—"friendship" is referred to a *topic* where henceforth the substitutive character of the relation—one might almost say its "formal" character—gains the upper hand: what should be recognized now is essentially the "circulation" of the figures, the impersonal exchange of phantasms, outside affectivity properly so-called: "This releases me from the field of affectivity—which cannot be spoken *without embarrassment*, since it belongs to the order of the imaginary" (*RB*, 65). We are on the spinning-wheel! Sometimes it whirs to the left; sometimes to the right; it goes now gee, now haw. Barthes "oscillates" between these two "postures," which, as we shall see, are not comfortable; he continues to come and go from one friend to another, or to revolve about the mother:

> I should therefore like the speaking and the listening that will be interwoven here to resemble the comings and goings of a child playing beside his mother, leaving her, returning to bring her a pebble, a piece of string, and thereby tracing around a calm center a whole locus of play within which the pebble, the string come to matter less than the enthusiastic giving of them. (*L*, 476–477)

Like this "child," Barthes constantly goes back and forth not only between "friends" and the atopic space to which they are supposed to refer but also between the "friends" and his mother, who, from a certain point of view, also defines a space to which "friends," close as they may be, cannot have access. In the same text, Barthes will call this gesture a "loosening method": namely, a method that "can really bear only on the means of loosening, baffling, or at the very least, of lightening this power" (*L*, 476), the constraining, even "alienating" (in a sense to be defined), power of language.

Meanwhile, since writing remains the very relay of desire, Barthes will continue to write essays—mirrors in which a "thought" constantly obsessing the later Barthes will be reflected: is a thought (proceeding) from the body possible? Or more precisely: if it is always my body that interprets the world, and if each body is multiple, what happens to the particularity or the identity of the subject?

This leads us to another series of related questions that allow us to situate more satisfactorily what is at stake in these later texts: what is a thought worth if it must be constrained to the words of the tribe? Or better: if the utilization of language in general seeps through us from "gregarious" life-style and morality, what can be the minimum conditions for singular "thought"? The new theme of "morality" will ensue directly from these general considerations, which Barthes neither invents nor combines. He contents himself, rather, with "translating" them; he enjoys "deporting" them for his needs (*RB*, 58). Thus it should not be surprising that the subject (of interpretation) itself comes to constitute an interpretation – or, as Barthes puts it: a "fiction"! – and that this interpretation implies a new "ethics." Let us try to situate the plurality of perspectives brought into play by Barthes in his recasting of (ethical) questions regarding language and the constitution of the subject.

A "euphoric" text founded on the pleasure and bliss (*jouissance*) of reader and writer, the Barthesian text is the least "reactive" text imaginable: it ignores stasis – "station" – or arrest, even those of "meditation"! It is uniquely animated by an insatiable *Will to Bliss* "exceeding" any "subject" and making all closure (of meaning) impossible:

> The brio of the text (without which, after all, there is no text) is its will to bliss: just where it *exceeds* demand, transcends prattle, and whereby it attempts to *overflow*, to break through the constraint of adjectives – which are those doors of language through which the ideological and the imaginary come flowing in. (*PT*, 13–14, emphasis mine)

Why then this insistence on/of friendship in Barthes's work? What can be its ultimate "signification" since this is obviously *not* a "pacificatory" theme?

By describing certain formal "procedures" at work in the essayistic writing of the later Barthes, I have already sketched an initial embryonic response (admittedly quite formal) to these questions: a subtly perfected turbine or paddle-wheel, essayistic writing is meant to draw up the most sophisticated reader and make him enter into the shimmering round of its "precious" signifiers (a unique round in each instance!). It is true that not everyone will be taken in *always and at every moment*, but the text is made in such a way that *none* can leave unscathed at the end: drawn from texts and from beings who are *loved*, it is written so that (always) at one moment or another and provided only that he agrees to read it, the "amorous" reader will fall upon a signifier, an interlude, a turn of thought that pleases him. And that is all the essayist seeks: the essay "floats," as Barthes says; it turns ceaselessly, waiting for the reader to "fall": seduced! The Barthesian text "cruises"; it loves its readers (one by one): "without equality, (but also) without in-difference."[71]

Oscillation

But it goes without saying that this movement of formalization – or better, perhaps, of "vicarious substitution" – this mad round that Barthes sometimes relates to the game of "pass the slipper" has nothing "formal" about it in the ordinary sense of the term. In any case it is not made to foreclose the eruption of the "grain" of things and voices or the very "flesh" of the beings that surround us and nourish our desires and our imaginary. In his late writings, it appears, Barthes begins to experience an increasingly imperative movement of "oscillation" – a word borrowed from Nietzsche via Klossowski—that leads to a radical challenging of the "position of the subject" in the general economy of the work in progress: it is as if the movement situated until then at a purely "abstract" and "intertextual" level—namely, the circulation of identificatory "roles" and "postures" from one "subject" to an "other"—is abruptly accelerated. The "masks" begin to parade by at remarkable speed and constantly question both the identity of the subject (Barthes) with himself and his internal "cohesion": that is to say, the cohesion of his Self—an instance more and more problematized in a "dramatic" mode, in the sense given this term by Bataille—with what he understands in the category (of) Body: his "unique" body.

As is often the case in Barthes, the general configuration of the "movement" (of "translation") that I note here is given to us not in a text directly concerned with himself, but rather in a text focusing on a "beloved" author. In a text devoted specifically to "oscillation" in Sollers—a Sollers read, as we shall see, through Nietzsche!—Barthes begins by introducing the notion of oscillation (opposed to "hesitation"), which he presents from the outset as the instrument of *the most radical* questioning of the "traditional role of the intellectual," only to go immediately to what he calls "the frantic music of oscillation" that any "devotion" to writing cannot fail to provoke. Immediately thereafter appears this cursory remark of capital interest to us:

> It (oscillation) seems to pass through *a sort of panic of the subject*, its surrender multiple, incessant, *and seemingly tireless.* We witness a mad *contest* between the "inconclusiveness" of attitudes—exaggerated ones, no doubt, but whose succession is always open ("I don't have anything definitive")—and the weight of the Image, which invincibly tends to become solid; for the destiny of the Image is immobility. (*SE*, 88)

Those who have read and considered, if only briefly, that fine book of Pierre Klossowski's, *Nietzsche et le cercle vicieux*, are sure to be struck by the movement of "translation" (of certain approaches and assumptions in Klossowski's book) that is at work here: proceeding from Sollers' work, writing on Sollers' work, Barthes cannot fail to summon a "register"—a "music of thought-words"!—that he borrows as is, from another context (another body [*corps*] or, if you like, another *corpus*) notably that of the Nietzsche of the "euphoria of Turin," the Nietzsche that Klossowski portrays as prey to the most wild fluctuations and "oscillations" of the "self," highly dangerous to his mental health. True, what Nietzsche is fomenting is nothing less than generalized "combat" against "culture"! One question now becomes vital: To what type of *necessity* does such a "translation" correspond? And before that, perhaps: *What then is effectively "translated"?* This "question" in itself would require a specialized work; but having raised it, I mean to provide certain of the elements that will make it possible to at least "situate" its place of inscription in Barthes's work.

To answer this difficult question—for it will help us to understand the nature of the seemingly contradictory "gesture" that makes Barthes oscillate between a "formalizing" movement that inscribes him in an ever changing circle of "friends" (of their "multiple" text!) and the movement that appears to be one of "abstinence" and retreat in which the "idiosyncratic" character of his "humors" (of his Body) becomes the object of his impossible quest—we must reconsider certain aspects of the text (*corpus*) that Barthes "translates." As I have already suggested, what henceforth "works" on Barthes's writing in an "underlying" but neither secret nor "unconscious" manner is, so far as I can see, Klossowski's interpretation of the posthumous fragments of the "late" Nietzsche and the to say the least "unconventional" inferences he draws from them. Because it plays an altogether central role, I think it useful to give, at least in part, an extract from one of the pivotal texts for Klossowski's approach (and, I think, for Barthes's as well): it is the extraordinary letter that Nietzsche wrote to Carl Fuchs on December 14, 1887:

> for I am, almost without willing it but in accordance with an inexorable necessity, right in the midst of settling my accounts with men and things and making a deposition *ad acta* [for the record] concerning my whole life hitherto. Almost everything I do now is a matter of drawing the final line. *In recent years, the vehemence of my inner oscillations has been terrifying*; now that I must make the transition to a new and higher form, I need above all a new estrangement, a still higher depersonalization. So it is of the greatest importance for me to know what and *who* are still left me.
>
> What age am I? I do not know—any more than I could say to what extent I might still be young. (Nietzsche, quoted by Klossowski, 311)

Except for the notation on the vehemence of the "inner oscillations" disturbing Nietzsche's thought, in this text we seem to be at the opposite pole from everything generally associated with Barthes's name: here, the Nietzschean pathos is too "marked" for a tie to be established, let us say, with the author of *A Lover's Discourse* or *Camera Lucida*. However, by carefully reading the text and, above all, situating it *in the context* that Klossowski so brilliantly reconstitutes for us, we discover certain obsessive, truly Barthesian themes: first, that absence of "will" and the concomitant "inexorable necessity" that demands (of the scriptor) a "settling of accounts with men and things." We need but think of the "combat" Barthes wages not only against the Image in general but also against the Image made of him, and of the fierce battle he wages against Meaning—meanings—that "set" too quickly and make all "thought of becoming" impossible (*PT*, 60, for example); we need but think, above all, of the increasing necessity in Barthes's writings to balance his accounts, to recapitulate (himself), to trace lines of demarcation between his work and that of others, between his body and that of others (including his "friends"); finally, we need but think of the major "motif" of battle against "arrogant" discourses, against the political and psychoanalytic "gendarmes," in short, against all discourses of "mastery"! What is deceptive is that the "translation" is not "servile." For Barthes, it is not a matter of transposing Nietzsche or adapting him to some philosophic or literary strategy, but rather of taking aslant this discourse which, as I shall try to show, will turn out to be closer to his personal preoccupations than he himself could ever have imagined. So close, moreover, that from a certain point of view, it is rather Barthes's text which, at another level of the spiral, is "taken" in the abrasive economy of the Nietzschean text: it is the biter bitten! Barthes begins by "flirting," as he puts it, with Nietzsche—whom he admits having read only late via Deleuze and Klossowski. But as relations are clarified, the entire economy of his work is "overwhelmed" in every sense of the term:

> I had my head full of Nietzsche, whom I had just been reading; but what I wanted, what I was trying to collect, was a song of sentence-ideas; the influence was purely prosodic. (*RB*, 107).

As we know, Barthes liked to recall that he had always written "to order": a word that was too often interpreted solely in mundane terms, but that can reflect another kind of "order" as well, an internal "exigency" that is no longer susceptible to a "historical" explanation: doesn't Barthes speak of his "devotion" to writing? Hasn't he constantly affirmed that his "work" proceeds by "conceptual infatuations" or by "amorous fits" (*RB*, 110)? Immediately following the publication of *S/Z*, this aspect, among other things, causes him to increasingly "implicate" the (texts of) "friends" in the wake (or the oscillations) of his writing: theater, fragment, Image, novelizing, Japan, music, the Self—a whole series of "themes," which, though not "novelties" for his pen, are nonetheless re-evaluated and re-inscribed in the ever changing body of reflections that become increasingly "individual" in manner. Nietzsche had "settled his account with men and things" in his *Ecce Homo*. Barthes will do the same—in parodic or "histrionic" fashion—by writing a book that will greatly infatuate the public while also bringing about considerable misunderstanding: *Roland Barthes by Roland Barthes*! Nor will it be long before Barthes sets down *ad acta* what had only been his 'hitherto' in the book in which, perhaps for the first time, he ventures to write "openly" of the "vehemence of his inner oscillations"): *Camera Lucida*.

In citing Nietzsche's letter to Carl Fuchs, I had only to put into context the "theme" that Barthes, retranslating from Nietzsche (via Klossowski's interpretation) "applies" to Sollers' work. It was necessary to go back to one of the "sources"—I don't say to the "origin"!—that triggered the mechanism of "translation." But it is clear that when it comes to considering the economy of the (new) "subject" of writing and its atopic circulation in the fragmentary space of the modern text, Barthes does not refer (solely) to this letter taken in isolation but rather to all the upheavals that it presupposes in Nietzsche's life and thought.

Since it is out of the question here to take into account all of the elements at stake in this intertextual "exchange," I shall content myself with considering the one that seems to have been the "triggering mechanism": namely, the renewed conception of the sign and Image in relation to the question of "subject."

First, *images*;—to explain how images are born in the mind. Then words applied to images. Finally, *concepts* possible only on the basis of *words*. (Nietzsche, cited by Klossowski, 316)

To bring to light what I consider absolutely essential in understanding the "later" Barthes, I would have to cite or recapitulate the totality of Klossowski's interpretation. For my purpose, I will only "summarize" its general movement and quote the two or three passages that seem to bear *directly* upon what Barthes endeavors to consider when borrowing the notion of "oscillation" from Nietzsche (once more, via the reading proposed by Klossowski!).

As a preliminary remark about this text—and the other texts from among Nietzsche's posthumous writings that follow in its train—let us note that it is inscribed in a context where, confronted as he says by his "interior oscillations," Nietzsche keeps questioning himself about (the impossibility of) his "identity": and generally, about the always "fortuitous" character of identification with a "character," a "self," that is *given* to us ONCE AND FOR ALL! As we know, for Nietzsche this "problematic"—lived in the dramatic mode—is inseparable from the confrontation with "friends" and those close to him: Fuchs, but also Lou-Andréas Salomé, Paul Rée, and Strindberg. His letters show him to be continuously attached to redefining a new version of "fatality" but also increasingly preoccupied with the question of his "idiosyncrasy." In one sense, *Ecce Homo* is merely an "inspired" transcription of what Nietzsche discovers in fear and trembling: "the absolute certainty about what I am was projected on *some accidental reality*—the truth about me spoke from some gruesome depth" (*Ecce Homo*, 275).[72]

But what is interesting here is that this "revelation" is contemporaneous with a radical questioning of the transparency of language. In fact, far from being the mere representative of a thing, idea, or representation passing through an already constituted consciousness or "subject," the code of signs of natural language and the system of "images"(!) that it bears are given as so many "abbreviations," as Nietzsche puts it, of (pulsional) movements of the body that no longer necessarily belong to a "self" or to a "subject" that are transparent to themselves. Nietzsche will thus propose a new "theory" of the subject—a new "model"—where henceforth "impulsions," desires as forces of non-speech and as unrepresentable "representatives" of an impossible "center" will determine all attempts to account for the general economy of the thinking and desiring subject. Clearly, one of the consequences of such a displacement is the redefining of the subject's "role" and "place," but the chief consequence is the birth of a new "continent" (a new "code," as Klossowski puts it).

From the moment when the "impulsions" assume command, it is less a question of understanding what moves the subject on the basis of conscious representations—that is, on the basis of (fixed) signs in everyday language—than (reversing the schema) of questioning the transparency and stability of each "cogitant" instance. Henceforth, Nietzsche tries to "think" from a radical reversal of perspectives: namely, from what he calls the "unintelligible depth" or the "Self" (*Selbst*). Thus we understand the nature of the "combat" that Nietzsche wages against the necessity of language and the system of "designations"—in Barthesian terms, of "Images" and/or of "Stereotypes"[73]—that it commands. Being merely the fortuitous product of the always "arbitrary" intervention—in the "political" sense of the term—of gregarious "values" borne by language, the subject must be entirely reconsidered: "Man," as Nietzsche will say in a formula that has not always been well understood, must be "overcome"! Here is how Klossowski renders this displacement, a rendering that must be given *in extenso*, for it constitutes an essential aspect of the "text" that Barthes in turn transposes for his own purposes:

> "*The contradiction is not between the 'true' and the 'false,' but between the abbreviations of signs and the signs*"—that is to say, the *impulsions* that collide with and interpret each other according to their fluctuations of intensity and, at the level of organized beings, the *gestures* create *forms* according to those movements and gestures and are led astray by this invention of signs that fix them by means of *abbreviation*. For in abridging them, these signs reduce them—apparently suspend their fluctuation *once and for all*: but in the interval of the (invariable) signs of language, the pulsional intensity can never be designated in other than an intermittent and arbitrary fashion by these abbreviations: their sphere of activity constitutes itself as meaning only if they choose for their goal this designated abbreviation and end in a combination of *units*. The former thus forms a declaration that sanctions the *fall of intensity*. . . . The intensities (of pulsion and repulsion) do not achieve signification unless they are first *reduced* by the abbreviative system to the *intentional* states of the subject. The latter henceforth *thinks* or *believes that he thinks* according to whether he feels *threatened* or *assured* in his persistence—specifically that of his intellect; which is never anything but *repulsion* for everything that could destroy the cohesion between the subject and the abbreviative system. . . . But how is thought possible if not because the fluctuations of intensity incessantly thwart their "*abbreviation*"? *We do not have a language to express what is constantly evolving*, says Nietzsche. (Klossowski, 78–80)

Let us now reread the text on "oscillation" in Sollers (or everything that in *The Pleasure of the Text* or *Roland Barthes*, for example, touches in some degree upon what Barthes calls a [new] "materialist theory of the subject"). We cannot help but be struck by the similarity in theoretical approach, as well as by the "affects" and "pathos" that come into play: it is certain, in any event, that whenever the "responsibility" of the modern text—its "ethical" import and the "morality" it implies—must be determined with some precision, Barthes always relies on Nietzsche.[74] But why does this insistent, systematic "phenomenon" always occur via someone else? Why must this problem always be advanced in disguise—sometimes so well disguised that it becomes unrecognizable? To answer this type of question, perhaps it would be better to reverse the terms by asking this: Why is it necessary to don a "mask" in order to speak of what in itself is perceived as irreducible—in Barthesian terms: "intractable"—namely, the body, "my unique body"?

Between what makes the "self" into a "unique" subject and what, stemming from other subjects (from other texts), makes the self into an arbitrary configuration open to revision, Barthes hesitates—he "oscillates." As he himself says: though he in fact can experience this slipping (from one desire to another, one infatuation to another, etc.), he "cannot conceptualize it"! *It floats!* At the end of each "phase" (*RB*, 145), Barthes always encounters a subject that is "anachronic," "adrift":

> Whenever I attempt to "analyze" a text which has given me pleasure, it is not my "subjectivity" I encounter but my "individuality," the given which makes my body separate from other bodies and appreciates its suffering or its pleasure: it is my body of bliss I encounter. And this body of bliss is also my historical subject; *for it is at the conclusion of a very complex process* of biographical, historical, sociological, neurotic elements (education, social class, childhood configuration, etc.) that I control the *contradictory interplay* of (cultural) pleasure and (non-cultural) bliss, and that I write myself as a subject *at present out of place, arriving too soon or too late* (this *too* designating neither regret, fault, nor bad luck, but merely calling for a non-site): anachronic *subject*, adrift. (*PT*, 62–63, emphasis mine)

As can be seen, it is unnecessary to "force" Barthes's texts to trace the movement of "oscillation" I evoked earlier. But in reading the text with a "sympathetic" eye (in the sense that we speak of sympathetic ink), we readily realize that the "nullity" that (provisorily) strikes the subject who writes these lines is justified only as the rehearsal of a scene wherein what is playing has already been played. Indeed, what is the problem set forth? Neither more nor less than this: how to restore in the "singular"—namely, to my body—the attributes of its singularity, by means of language (the language common to everyone)? How to translate the inexchangeable—my body of bliss—in the terms of gregarious communication? Or again, how to give the uncultural mutism—of my body of bliss—a "voice" if whenever I read (the text of others), whenever I write, it is always the language of others that I encounter?

What clearly emerges is that the way in which Barthes questions and discusses the "reading" and "analysis" of texts and of the body is only one aspect of his questioning himself about himself. But on this terrain, there is at least someone who preceded him and this is the one who from *The Pleasure of the Text* on will not stop haunting his text: the Nietzsche of the "Eight Capital Questions": [75]

> Is one a *problem* or a *solution*? . . . in perfect fashion if the task is minimal, imperfect if the goal is extraordinary? Is one *authentic* or merely an *actor*, authentically an actor or merely parodying an actor, is one the representative of something or that which is represented? . . . "someone" or a rendezvous of someone. . . . Is one unaccomplished because one has appeared too soon or because one has appeared too late? Is it by nature that one says "yes" and that one says "no," or rather does one only form a motley mixture of colors like a peacock's tail? (Nietzsche, cited by Klossowski, 120–121)

It would be difficult to read this text without finding in it all the accents and themes that will increasingly inhabit the Barthesian text: What is *singular*? What is *gregarious*? What makes *my* body into a "unique" body? These are Nietzschean questions that Barthes retranslates by increasingly adopting a mode of writing— the fragment, the aphorism—which had become inseparable from Nietzsche's work. But even though "translated," the criteria of what is "singular" and of what is "gregarious" remain the same:

Singular	*Gregarious*
body (inexchangeable)	self (exchangeable)
non-language	language
individual	subjectivity
Bliss (*Jouissance*)	Pleasure
"unculture"	Culture
writerly	readerly, etc.
New	Old (*PT*, 40–41)
punctum	*studium*, etc.

By adding to this schema the categories of decadence and blossoming, of morbid and healthy, or of weak and powerful, you will confront the schema of principal criteria developed by Nietzsche in order to put the text of occidental metaphysics into perspective. Refusing to enter the *Machè* of philosophical debates, Barthes "translates" for himself—that is to say, for literature—"criteria" that, despite coming to him from "elsewhere," nonetheless possess a resonance that goes back to the most "intimate" experience. Whatever form the paradigm takes, it always refers to the same problem: What in the subject who reads, who writes, who finds bliss, determines her singularity? Now to speak (of) this, we must use the common language, and therefore "difference," the body as "irreducible difference" must necessarily be erased. At this point, we can better understand the "role" in which Barthes (in friendly fashion) casts Sollers' text: faced with an author who systematically questions the economy of the "subject" of the enunciation, who is *at the same time* a "friend" who in no small way contributed to making him known and, from a certain perspective, transforming him into a mythic "Image" – I am thinking of the Sollers of the special issue of *Tel Quel* on "R.B." – Barthes is sent back to a "topic" that can be "translated" on the scene of language and become "communicable" only by being (re)lived in the mode of repetition of an "other" scene. As Barthes says in a striking passage:

> Not believing in the separation of affect and sign, of the emotion and its theater, he could not *express* an admiration, an indignation, a love, for fear of signifying it badly. Thence, the more moved he was, the more lusterless. His "serenity" was merely the constraint of an actor who does not come on stage lest he perform too badly. (*RB*, 177)

Hardly being more explicit, I would say that Barthes, referred by Sollers' text to that which arouses the strongest "emotion" (phantasm) in him, finds not a scapegoat in Nietzsche but the relay of his secret phantasm: "Incapable of making himself convincing to himself, yet it is the very conviction of others which in his eyes makes them into creatures of theater and fascinates him." (ibid.) Consequently, what seems to determine "in depth" Barthes's relation to "friends," to those close to him, and perhaps, as we shall see, to the "other" in general, is first of all a large circulation of shared "affects," "words," "tastes," and "phantasms" always accompanied by a major risk: that, precisely, of becoming the prisoner of these Images – of being "ninnified" by them, as Gombrowicz would say – in short, of being "caught" in a network of images, "words," that quickly replaces the earlier emotions and affects (judged more *authentic* according to a quite Nietzschean process) *with their reductive "abbreviations"* (from the many to the *one*): that is to say, by the words of the tribe, of all and everyone. As Klossowski puts it so well:

> The word, as soon as it signifies an emotion, makes its signification
> pass for identical to the experienced emotion itself, which is strong only
> at the moment when there was no word. The signified emotion, weaker
> than the insignificant, unsignified emotion. (316)

Wanting to communicate from the non-communicable – his "body" – and having to discuss Sollers' work – namely, a work that touches him and always mobilizes the imaginary—Barthes thus is quite naturally (?) forced to abandon the Image where it is sticky and "obsolete" and to use a "unique" Sign—or a name—that by its intrinsic power would enable us to supplement the lack of origin and the absence of any (originary) foundation of the subject "Barthes": in short, not to justify, but at least to make possible or viable a "writing" that is (as it already knows) an orphan! As Unique Sign, the Name of Nietzsche will no longer "represent" the return to an origin or the establishment of a foundation, but literally the "invention" of a new (language) "game"—the penultimate: the return of the subject (but) as fiction. Is it by chance that—immediately after quoting a text in which Nietzsche displays "interpretation" as the Will to Power and as a "passional" process—Barthes writes:

> Then perhaps the subject returns, not as illusion, but as fiction. A certain pleasure is derived from a way of imagining oneself as individual, of inventing a final, rarest fiction: *the fictive identity*. This fiction is no longer the illusion of a unity; on the contrary, it is the theater of society in which we *stage our plural*: our pleasure is individual—but not personal. (PT, 62, emphasis mine)

"Inventing a final, rarest fiction: the fictive identity!" Thanks to the Unique Sign, Barthes can bring into play his strongest thought (which he believes he has found again in Asiatic thought, in the Tao for example): no longer having to interpret in conceptual terms, that is, being liberated from the "ennui" represented in the old configuration of his thought by the necessity "to cipher" the impulsional movements, the flushes of pleasure traversing the text, by relating them to designations in everyday language and, consequently, by "obliterating" their intrinsic *force* His position strengthened by what the Unique Sign spares him from having to "conceptualize," Barthes follows a "path" brilliantly traced by Nietzsche before him, and, for a time, concentrates on "retranslating" the assumptions of the Nietzschean "semiotics" for his personal "needs": namely, converting the signs coming from consciousness—indeed, the signs constituting it! —into an impulsional semiotics (that of the "body of bliss," as Barthes says). Such is, it seems, the meaning of the (new) christening of semiology in the "Inaugural Lecture" of 1977. Like the phoenix, semiology is reborn from its ashes, but this time as *semiotropy*. *I die a fox, I am reborn a hawk*, so runs a sentence from the *Egyptian Book of the Dead*. It is not surprising to see semiology release (itself from) a theory of the sign which, though not enunciating itself in the exact terms of Nietzschean pathos, nevertheless retains the "elegance" given it by Nietzschean histrionics. And this new semiology can recount splendidly the "tropism" that the Unique Sign induces in the "person" it elects:

> This negative semiology is an active semiology: it functions outside death. I mean by this that it does not rest on a "semiophysis," an inert naturalness of the sign, and that it is also not a "semioclasty," a destruc-

tion of the sign. Rather, to continue the Greek paradigm, it is a *semiotropy*; turned toward the sign, this semiology is captivated by and receives the sign, treats and, if need be, imitates it as an imaginary spectacle.

The semiologist is, in short, an artist. . . . He plays with signs as with a conscious decoy, whose fascination he savors and wants to make others savor and understand. . . . This semiology (need I specify once more: the semiology of the speaker) is not a hermeneutics: it paints more than it digs. . . . Its objects of predilection are texts of the Image-making process: narratives, images, portraits, expressions, idiolects, passions, structures which play simultaneously with an appearance of verisimilitude and with an uncertainty of truth. (*L*, 474–475)

And Barthes concludes:

I should like to call "semiology" the course of operations during which it is possible—even called for—to play with the sign as with a painted veil, or again, with a fiction. (ibid.)

Later in the text, Barthes will propose not a teaching *on* phantasm or *the* phantasmatic, but a "phantasmatic" teaching (*L*, 477) which he "justifies" by referring to Michelet:

It is to a fantasy, spoken or unspoken, that the professor must annually return, at the moment of determining the direction of his journey. He thereby turns from the place where he is expected, the place of the Father, who is always dead, as we know. For only the son has fantasies; only the son is alive. (*L*, 477)

At the moment of "determining the direction of his journey," the professor Barthes feels himself locked up somewhere—in the Institution, Images, duties, lectures—and fails to be at one with himself: the messages sent him by the Nietzschean text—the prisoner of its own secret phantasm and prey to the "same" Sign—remain unintelligible to him: he may understand the text's assumptions, but he can no longer conceptualize the text. As far back as he can go, the fixity of the code of signs closes in upon him—freezes him—and what belongs to him exclusively constantly remains *outside*, outside him, in the time described by the universe (of signs) and recounted by the history (of literature): the memory that outlives men is my mother and the *chaos* that centers upon itself is my father:

I am, to express it in the form of a riddle, already dead as my father, while as my mother I am still living and becoming old. (*Ecce Homo*, 222)

The father, dead very early (in the war), was lodged in no memorial or sacrificial discourse. By maternal intermediary his memory—never an oppressive one—merely touched the surface of childhood with an almost silent bounty. (*RB*, 15)

Don't they understand me?—Orpheus facing Dionysus . . . !

I cannot write myself. What, after all, is this "I" who would write himself? Even as he would enter into the writing, the writing *would take the wind out of his sails, would render him null and void*—futile; a gradual dilapidation would occur, in which the other's image, too, would be gradually involved (to write on something is to outmode it), a disgust whose conclusion could only be: what's the use? What obstructs amorous writing is the illusion of expressivity: as a writer, or assuming myself to be one, I continue to fool myself as to the effects of language: I do not know that the word "suffering" expresses no suffering and that, consequently, to use it is not only to communicate nothing but even, and immediately, to annoy, to irritate (not to mention the absurdity). *Someone would have to teach me that one cannot write without burying "sincerity" (always the Orpheus myth: not to turn back)*. What writing demands, and what any lover cannot grant it without laceration, is to sacrifice a little of his Image-repertoire [*Imaginaire*], and to assure thereby, through his language, the assumption of a little reality. (*LDF*, 98, emphasis mine)

To try to write love is to confront the muck of language: that region of hysteria where language is both too much and too little, excessive (by the limitless expansion of the ego, by *emotive submersion*) and impoverished (by the codes on which love diminishes and levels it). Faced with the death of his baby son, *in order to write* (if only scraps of writing), Mallarmé submits himself to parental division:

> *Mère, pleure*
> *Moi, je pense.*
>
> Mother, weep
> While I think.

But the amorous relation has made me into an atopical subject— undivided: *I am my own child: I am both mother and father (of myself, of the other): how would I divide the labor?* (ibid., 99, emphasis mine)

As my mother, I am still living and becoming old. Not in the sense that, through symmetry, the Mother represents blossoming. Nietzsche substitutes himself, always substituted himself not for his father beside his mother—following the Oedipal schema—but inversely, for his mother beside his father, as being his own mother. He explains this later as his self-cure. (Klossowski, 258)

"Always the Orpheus myth: not to turn back"! But as the story recounts: Orpheus ends up turning back. In fact, everything in the "myth" says that one (always) turns back: towards "friends," the texts one has written, the (always) dead father, the (aging) mother. When all has been said and done, his head is "confused": "On a certain kind of work, on a certain kind of subject . . . on a certain day of life itself, he would like to be able to post as a motto this old-wives' remark: 'My head is confused' (let us imagine a language in which the set of grammatical categories would sometimes force the subject to speak *in the aspect of an old woman*" (*RB*, 176, emphasis mine). But what happens when Orpheus "turns back" *towards himself*? What "Image" is sent back to him? And in what mirror?

Each time dialogue occurs in an exchange of (commissioned) texts or of words (in an interview) with the others – friends – a gap appears between what is effectively experienced (felt) and what is expressed (proffered). The mere use of the *word* ("suffering," for example) not only expresses "nothing at all" (no suffering), but in a general way makes "communication" impossible: "conceived" in order "to express" the "generality," language will henceforth be conceived as the privileged instrument of what is constituted by foreclosing that which makes me a singular being, my "genuineness." To speak (to write) will henceforth be equivalent to giving up for lost what sets me apart, offering up in sacrifice a little of my imaginary. This new conception of language – which systematically comes to light from *The Pleasure of the Text* onwards and will be developed in Barthes's work and life – determines in depth the nature of the "relations" Barthes will maintain with his circle: (even) his "friends" will show themselves incapable of following the implications of such a theoretical position through to its logical conclusion; they still grant too much to "language" and do not "reflect" enough (on) the emotional genesis of thought: in short, on what Barthes henceforth calls the Body, his body. When he invites them to consider this problem with him, he does so by urging them to turn their attention to his own prior emotion – that is, to the always "unique" character of the affections of his body:

His friends on *Tel Quel*: their originality, their truth (aside from their intellectual energy, their genius for writing) insist that they *must agree to speak a common, general, incorporeal language*, i.e., political language, although each of them speaks it with his own body. – Then why don't you do the same thing? – Precisely, no doubt, because I do not have the same body that they do; *my body cannot accommodate itself to generality, to the power of generality which is in language*. – Isn't that an individualistic view? Wouldn't one expect to hear it from a Christian – a notorious anti-Hegelian – such as Kierkegaard? (*RB*, 175, emphasis mine).

If the first proposition – my body is not the same as yours – can actually be associated without too much distortion with Kierkegaard (the author of *Repetition*, for example), the second proposition — associating language with "generality" — is more difficult to attribute to Kierkegaard without further ado. In any case, it cannot be assimilated to an "individualistic" view, which would, moreover, be "Christian"! Reading this text, one would be more likely to think spontaneously of Nietzsche, the Nietzsche who, on the eve of his "dissolution," proposed a new "model" of "thought" (of the body) on the basis of a "semiotics" of non-speech: one might say, of "gestures of the idea" and "sensual objects" — at this early date!

Why then this shifting? Why this sort of denial? Nietzsche said it is not the lie that kills, but truth. Knowing the truth, since he on many occasions proffered it "elsewhere" — namely, that our "bliss" is "individual" and not "personal" — Barthes provisorily "denies" it, defers it till "later": this does not prevent him from being constantly occupied by the same problems (*underlying* the type of relationships he maintains with his "friends," but also with the Nietzschean "intertext"): the subject, like "desire," is formed and comes undone according to the "receptivity and acceptance of "friends" — without friends, would I still have the courage to write? — but also because of the "arbitrary" character of the encounter with the texts and languages that give me pleasure and "seduce" me. The "subject" (of writing and of reading) will thus always be apprenticed or "in waiting" in a (textual) interregnum:

> It is not apprenticeship which never ends, but rather desire. My work seems to be made up of a succession of "disinvestments"; there is only one object from which I have never disinvested my desire: language: language is my *objet petit a*. From *Degree Zero* on, I have chosen language to love — and, of course, to detest at the same time: altogether trusting and altogether mistrusting it; but *my methods of approach, dependent on what was being expressed all around me and what exercised its particular fascinations on me, could change*, that is to say: to try one's hand at something [*s'essayer*], to please, that is to transform oneself, to abandon oneself: it is as if one always loved the same person, but kept trying out new erotics with that person. ("Responses," in *Tel Quel* 47, 100)

This was said in 1971: a still happy year in which Barthes's conception of language has not as yet taken the shape — so badly misunderstood for not having been related to its undermining "source"! — that the "encounter" with Nietzsche would give it: the language is still Lacanian — "it is my *objet petit a*" — it has not yet become "fascist." But this is because the essential stake at that "period" was still the deconstruction of the "subject" of the "idealist" conception of language. But presently — essentially from *The Pleasure of the Text* onwards — it will no longer be the abstract reader given us by Doxa or Science that interests Barthes, but, the reader — and the writer as "lexeographer" — inasmuch as they (he) constitute(s) a particular body (of bliss): in other words, the *inexchangeable itself!*

Returning thus to the source of his "desire" — reading and writing — and to another level of the "spiral," Barthes touches upon a "reality" (*un réel*): the body as a heterotopical montage of (beloved) texts. "Intermingling of body and language: which comes first?" One's head is "confused." Consequently, it becomes easier to understand the importance that the "theme" of Nietzschean oscillation had for Barthes — close as it was to his own "experience" just then: no longer speaking as "subject," as Author, but above all, attentive to that which from the texts questions at every moment the cohesion of his present (?) Self with what he calls the Body, Barthes quite naturally comes *to repeat* the experience that Nietzsche had lived through before him: in a "mad" gesture, to try to translate the semiotics of consciousness — namely, the likes and dislikes, the phantasms, etc. — into an "impulsional semiotics." The last "theory" of the "Image" proceeds directly from this new imperative: to draw a (materialist) "theory" of the subject no longer from Reason or from the Idea (from the Concept), but from the "given" of "his" body henceforth conceived as a capacity of "resistance" to what, stemming from the Combat of Languages — that which Barthes calls *Machè* — tends to "freeze" it. Caught in the game of "leech-languages,"[76] the body adopts *reflexes* whose tendency will be domestication: by the (ready-made) Images that they carry along, these languages will elect (will maintain) *this* body only to make of it the *body of no one*: the "Guelph" spirit finally gets the upper hand over the "Ghibelline" spirit. The body as body is no longer synonymous with itself: the instrument of a consciousness henceforth purely "reactive," it literally becomes the homonym of the "person" Barthes transformed into an Image ("frozen").

Reflecting upon the desire which makes him write and think, Barthes discovers that he is caught in a body *that does not belong to him*: his "fear" — which is not pure "anguish" — he will interpret henceforth as the combat between an "unintelligible depth" (which he names the Body, "unreadable" in essence) and the, if not artificial, at least always *arbitrary* identity of the "subject." In any case, it is certain that Barthes in his "maturity"[77] is more and more convinced that the body proper is never anything but the fortuitous encounter of desires, of likes and dislikes, and (why not?) of contradictory Images and Phantasms that form a homogeneous whole — namely, a subject that is transparent and identical to itself — only on a functional base ("utilitarian," in the sense Nietzsche gives to this term) that is *overdetermined socially, culturally, and historically*. In other words (and such is the [secret] phantasm that Barthes "translates" from Nietzsche): If it were not for the *Machè* of languages and the omnipotence that it despotically exercises on us, it would not be a single body — and consequently a single "identity" and a single "history" once and for all — that we would be able to experience, but a multiplicity of bodies. Taking up a movement of thought similar in many aspects to the Nietzschean problematics of *Selbst* — as *Selbstsucht* (yearning for self, i.e., "selfishness") and as unconscious force that transcends consciousness and its representations — Barthes will attempt to make the wager that consists in lending a voice to the multiple body that he experiences in himself, by reading, by writing – beyond or rather this side of what he henceforth interprets as simple "fallout" that springs from the power of "leech-languages" on his "idiosyncrasy." Once the multiple Body is recognized as the product of "pulsions," of likes and dislikes – "enslaved, organized, hierarchized" by the *Machè* – all transparency with the Self (Barthes) will inevitably appear as a secondary and contingent formation: reference to the Body will consequently be used to stage a "thought" and a "writing" infinitely more vast than those which until then were arbitrarily merged with the subject R. B. such as in himself "friends" had for a time transformed him.

But thereafter, the "perspective" became completely transformed: it is now less a matter of exalting "one's" body – which one? – on the basis of an assured "selfish" (narcissistic) position, than of trying to give "place" to a "thought" that would speak the body (if possible) from a space of writing or of thought that would be liberated from Images, from Stereotypes (and therefore from language): it is a matter, in other words – in a movement of extraordinary "abstinence" – of restoring thought to the active forces that determine the Body as "reality" or "intractable" fact. The theme of significance – which Barthes significantly opposes to *écrivance* or as he puts it: "meaning insofar as it is sensually produced" (*PT*, 61) signifies precisely this: to lend "voice" to the Body amounts to imperiling the "subject's" transparency to itself and to questioning the cohesion that this "subject" maintains with that which proceeds from the Body as *Selbst*: neither consciousness nor Unconsciousness, but perhaps "Will to Power" (*PT*, 62)!

The Pleasure of the Text will be the first systematic attempt undertaken by Barthes to restore thought to "bodily" forces (to impulsions) (Klossowski, 57) and to go beyond the "reduced" (popular) conception of the body: specifically that which makes an entity of it, an entity opposed to the "soul." In writing *Roland Barthes*, Barthes does not try to say "who he is," but, quite the contrary, to bring to the fore the elements that justify the *fortuity* of his being. A pseudo-autobiography – a portrait of the "artist" as an old histrion – *Roland Barthes* will be conceived less to exalt an exemplary Self than to "describe the progressive release of an *idiosyncrasy at the expense of this self*, insofar as it imposes itself on this self, and disintegrates it into what it itself constitutes" (Klossowski, 323).

Proceeding from what he henceforth calls the Body – his body – as "eternal return" of an "impersonal" desire that always questions its own coherence, Barthes, in his turn, will come to a new conception (of the relation) of sign and of subject. Indeed, as soon as language is conceived as the instrument in us of an "alienation" that precludes our idiosyncrasy – such is the meaning of the remark: "Language . . . is neither reactionary nor progressive; it is quite simply fascist" (*L*, 461) – the question of "subject" becomes that of discourse: is there a possible discourse (a language) to speak (of) what, on this side of conscious representations and Images, can never be entirely suppressed: namely, the Body as unintelligible depth? As Klossowski, whom I must quote, says: "How would it [discourse] translate the arbitrary liberty of the unintelligible depth into persuasive constraint? Will discourse not be purely arbitrary? *Certainly, if the conceptual form is maintained!*" (Klossowski, 360)

In forming his notion of "gestures of the idea"—or of "intellectual objects"—Barthes tries to resolve this problem: writing "fragments," he wants to "render to the act of thinking itself its virtue of resisting all 'conceptualization' " and to maintain it this side of the "norms"—always "gregarious"—of language. The massive entrance of the fragment into Barthes's work after *S/Z* is directly "rooted" in Nietzsche: it becomes necessary because it alone can render an account of the play of antagonistic forces that in a "cyclic" manner question the identity of the subject "R.B." The fragment is the perfect instrument of the new "topic" because it adapts so well to the subject's eclipses or, if you like, to the subject as an "eclipse machine." Barthes's passion for the theater (Asiatic, in particular) has no other "justification": like the Oriental actor, the essayist will no longer seek to be *a* writer, he will not even seek to be *one*, but will try only to "combine" the signs that designate us as "figures" (falsely) "arrested," thus freeing us of the burden that such signs, when they are not viewed critically, impose on us.

> However, insofar as these signs (those conveyed by the Japanese actor) are extreme, not because they are bombastic (one sees that they are not so), but because they are intellectual—being, like writing, "the gesture of the idea"—they purify the body of all expressivity: one might say that by dint of being signs they exhaust meaning. (Barthes, *L'Empire des signes*, 95)

> At the crossroads of the entire *oeuvre*, perhaps the Theater: there is not a single one of his texts, in fact, which fails to deal with a certain theater, and spectacle is the universal category in whose aspect the world is seen. The theater relates to all the apparently special themes which pass and return in what he writes: connotation, hysteria, fiction, the image-repertoire, the scene, grace, the Orient, violence, ideology. (*RB*, 177)

When Barthes tries to recapitulate his itinerary and to bring to the fore certain of the elements that determine his "idiosyncrasy"—the special case "R.B."!—it is always to other figures, other names, other texts that he is endlessly referred—what the "reflecting" mirror of the Infinite Text (himself) sends back is not an "identity" (with himself) that has a univocal purpose, but an infinite "reflection," a perpetual linking of "phantasms which persist from age to age, often independently of the writings of the Author" (*RB*, 99). Instead of the "depth" of his own being—in Barthesian terms, instead of the *Abgrund!*—what he brings to light is always a "figure," or as he says an "intertext" (*RB*, 145), that makes him defer, makes him constantly put off till later, the moment of decision. No edification whatsoever: no more than a "stubborn swarm" (of representations, of desires, of phantasms):

> The Gidean *Abgrund*, the Gidean core, unchanging, still forms in my head a stubborn swarm. Gide is my original language, my *Ursuppe*, my literary soup. (*RB*, 99)

But writing this, Barthes secretly knows that the body (of texts) whose singularity he tries to delimit is the same body only insofar as the same Self can and wants to merge with it, with its "vicissitudes" (Klossowski, 55): now, as one of the texts I cited earlier clearly establishes (*PT*, 61) – there are numerous others – when Barthes tries his hand at analyzing a text that has succeeded in mobilizing the "depth" in him, it is never his subjectivity that he finds, but his "body of bliss" as already having been *lived!*, namely as a "historical subject." In other words, it is never any longer the subject (Barthes) who "chooses," but always the Body which, at the mercy of the fluctuations of the forces and the desires traversing it, presents itself as this particular desiring subject, this particular amorous subject!

In Memoriam

> The ages of the body, in reality, are merely *the impulsional movements that form it* and deform it and then tend to *abandon* it. But the pulsions, at first its resources, are equally a menace to its cohesion. Its purely functional cohesion, in the service of the identity of the self, is in this sense irreversible: the *ages* of the self are those of its cohesion, that is to say that the more this self begins to grow old in and with this body, the more it aspires to cohesion, the more too it seeks to find again its point of departure – and thus to *recapitulate* itself. The apprehension of physical disintegration demands a retrospective vision of one's own cohesion. Thus, because the *self*, product of the body, claims this body *as its own* and *cannot* create another for itself, the self, too, has its *irreversible* history.
>
> The identity of the self with that of its "own body" remains inseparable from a meaning formed by the *irreversible* course of a human life: thus meaning survives the self as its accomplishment. Whence the *immortality of meaning "once and for all."* (Klossowski, 55)

> Therefore, if I want to live, I must forget that my own body is historical. I must fling myself into the illusion that I am contemporary with the young bodies present before me, and not with my own body, my past body. In short, I must be periodically reborn. I must make myself younger than I am. At fifty-one, Michelet began his *vita nuova*, a new work, a new love. Older than he (you will understand that this

parallel is out of fondness), I too am entering a *vita nuova*, marked today by this new place, this new hospitality. I undertake therefore to let myself be borne on by the force of any living life, forgetfulness. This is an age at which we teach what we know. Then comes another age at which we teach what we do not know; this is called *research*. Now perhaps comes the age of another experience: that of *unlearning*, of yielding to the unforeseeable change which forgetting imposes on the sedimentation of the knowledges, cultures, and beliefs we have traversed." (*L*, 478)

Read in the light of *Camera Lucida*, the association I am suggesting here between the two texts I have just cited assumes the dimensions of a "poignant" and tragic event, for each, in its own way, seems to announce the next "destiny" or the final destination of the work to come: indeed, even if it is difficult to know its efficient "cause"—is it because he foresees the imminent death of his mother?—it is clear that from *The Pleasure of the Text* onward Barthes does not cease to recapitulate (himself) and to appeal to "friends." But it is striking that this profound movement proves inseparable from an acceleration of the "oscillations" to which Barthes is more and more frequently subject. From *The Pleasure of the Text* onward, the frantic round of figures that haunted the Barthesian text becomes increasingly subject to the necessity for taking bearings, seeing the way clear, drawing lines of demarcation—within, even, the circle of "friends." "My whole little universe in crumbs; at the center, what?" (*RB*, 93). (A summing-up immediately follows in the text.) *Punctum*: Do a summing-up [*une mise au point*] (of what touches me). Speak no further of what "pricks" me and touches me. Make the point, but also perhaps *at the same time* "reach" the point in Georges Bataille's sense:

> One only reaches the point by dramatizing it. Dramatizing is what the devout who follow the *Exercises of Saint Ignatius* do (*but not only those*). . . . In any case, we can only project the point-object through drama. I have had recourse to overwhelming images. In particular, I fixed the photographic image—or at any rate, the memory I have of it—of a Chinese who may have been tortured in my lifetime.
> (*L'Expérience interieure*, 184–85)

Camera Lucida will fix the photographic image of the "winter garden," it will seek to "reach" the point (*punctum*)—in proffering at least once that which in me does not partake of any Image!—by *dramatizing* things: by projecting the point-object (the absent mother) through drama, Barthes will try to track down ("once and for all"?) that in himself which belongs only to him and which dooms him to death. Forgetfulness, which as we know, was not long before what enabled me to read (*S/Z*, 18), forgetfulness as "the force of all living life," is no longer acceptable: once the mother is dead, "the science of the unique being" (*CL*, 71) becomes "impossible" (to defer):

> Once she was dead I no longer had any reason to attune myself to the progress of the superior Life Force (the race, the species). My particularity could never again universalize itself (unless, utopically, by writing, whose project henceforth would become the unique goal of my life). From now on I could no more than await my total, undialectical death. That is what I read in the Winter Garden Photograph. (*CL*, 72)

As long as his mother was living (present) it was not urgent, so to speak, for Barthes to speak his "particularity" (that would have been one more "image," and "emphatic," to boot): he knows that somewhere someone is waiting for him and loves him *for what he is* without needing to speechify or to theorize[78]: *sine medio*, such is the watchword of maternal love for Barthes. But each time that, as writer or "public" man, he enters the *Machè* of languages, each time he thus finds himself exposed to Images, the question of his idiosyncrasy resurfaces: it is like military service; I am obliged to comply with the Image. I cannot be "exempted." *Fort/Da*: each time he is obliged to enter the public arena, Barthes must abandon his "creation of self," be "frozen," become an Image, in short, a "non-person," a figure of fashion: "Fashion affects the body. By fashion I return in my text as farce, as caricature. A kind of collective 'id' replaces the image I thought I had of myself, and that 'id' is me" (*RB*, 146).

If, being "cultivated," the Image loosens its hold a bit and becomes more ethereal, it nevertheless remains an Image. Friendship will thus remain in the final instance on the side of the species, on the side of gregarious values and the Imaginary. Even with "friends," one must still speak the common, general, incorporeal language.

When Barthes bids them to think with him one last time, it is, above all, to *feel* with him; he is inviting them to experience his own prior emotion. For the last time. Still haunted by an image: that of Nietzsche weeping with pity as he throws himself on the neck of a beaten horse!

> I then realized that there was a sort of link (or knot) between Photography, madness, and something whose name I did not know. I began by calling it: the pangs of love. Was I not, in fact, in love with the Fellini automaton? Is one not in love with certain photographs? . . . Yet it was not quite that. It was a broader current than a lover's sentiment. In the love stirred by Photography (by certain photographs), another music is heard, its name oddly old-fashioned: Pity. I collected in a last thought the images which had "pricked" me (since this is the action of the *punctum*), like that of the black woman with the gold necklace and the strapped pumps. In each of them, inescapably, I passed beyond the unreality of the thing represented, I entered crazily into the spectacle,

into the image, taking into my arms what is dead, what is going to die, as Nietzsche did when, on January 3, 1889, he threw himself in tears on the neck of a beaten horse: gone mad for Pity's sake. (*CL*, 116–117)

Dying of not dying, Barthes dreams of forcing the doors of a "mystical" realm where he might consume himself, drown himself in love. Now, it is only at this cost—at the cost of his lucidity—that he thinks he can accede *to the extreme*. In the end, he no longer encounters a "music" (of word-thoughts), but Nietzsche's "air" as a "luminous shadow that accompanies his body": a simulacrum. Formulating to himself his phantasm (of death) by way of Nietzsche's, he can still, for a time, signify that which "pinpoints" him without disappearing into abstract generality. For once, perhaps, the instituted signs will have served to designate (against themselves) the most singular experience in the world.

By way of epilogue:

> If the phantasm is, for everyone, that which makes one a singular case, to defend oneself against the institutional signification given by the gregarious group, the singular case cannot help but have recourse to the simulacrum: namely, an equivalent for its phantasm as well as a token that makes possible a fraudulent exchange between the singular case and the gregarious generality. But if this exchange is fraudulent, it is because the generality, no less than the singular case, intends it to be: the singular case disappears as such as soon as it signifies what it is for itself: individuals have only their species to insure their intelligibility. Not only does the individual disappear as such as soon as he formulates his own phantasm for himself—for he can do so only by means of instituted signs—but he recognizes himself through these signs only by excluding himself at the same time from what becomes intelligible, exchangeable in him. (Klossowski, 367)

15. Coming to a Close

He often resorts to a kind of philosophy vaguely labeled *pluralism*.

Who knows if this insistence on the plural is not a way of denying sexual duality? The opposition of the sexes must not be a law of Nature; therefore, the confrontations and paradigms must be dissolved, both the meanings and the sexes be pluralized: meaning will tend toward its multiplication, its dispersion (in the theory of the Text), and sex will be taken into no typology. (*RB*, 69)

Taking the essay as the principal theme of a book was, in a certain way, a wager, because far from letting itself be enclosed by the limits of a determined *genre*, my object tended rapidly toward a maximal opening and went beyond any attempt to classify, reduce, or enclose. In fact, having considered the different types of approach in Montaigne's essays alone, we quickly became aware that the "boundaries" of the essay were not only "blurred" but were caught, rather, in a sort of perpetual mobility: no fixed sender, no unified subject or themes, and finally, no definite addressee. As unclassifiable text, the essay is the text that makes it difficult to answer the classic question: which genre? We do not know if it falls within the realm of poetics, rhetoric, aesthetics, history, or philosophy. Or in all these realms *simultaneously*.

In fact, in order to account for the economy of Montaigne's *Essays*, and through them for the specificity of this text apart, the *essay*, innumerable models that would have served as springboard have been invoked: Plato's dialogues—the aporetic dialogues in particular—the letters and epistles of Seneca and Pliny, the *Meditations* of Marcus Aurelius or the *Confessions* of Saint Augustine. This is the approach that erudite critics like Lukács and Pierre Villey, for example, have adopted. But by "dismantling" certain of the cogwheels at the origin of the efficacity of the essay, I have tried to show that despite the historical or descriptive interest of such an approach, reference to these models does not explain why this impossible text took so long to make its theoretical entrance into the hierarchy of genres.

While recapitulating this aspect of things—what, with Sollers, I shall call the "reflex of reduction" of the essay to "something else"—I saw the need to overturn perspectives and change the stakes, no longer asking whence the *Essays* came (the always pointless question of origins?), from which anterior genres? Or again: which "thought" (Is there only *one* thought for Montaigne or Barthes)? But rather: how does this work? What effects does this produce? According to which procedure?

In refusing to have recourse (solely) to Rhetoric, I wanted to avoid being forced once more to assign origins to the essay and thus be caught up again in the snares of an exegesis that—as I have said—though it may be necessary is not sufficient. What then clearly appeared is the false alternative in which classical literary criticism and Rhetoric have always engaged us as far as the essay is concerned: either it is a degenerate genre, a generic mishap, a formless text without borders, an abyss without differences and without specific properties; or else it is a rhetorically well-constructed text, clearly *individuated* and decodable—"readable," as Barthes said—a Form highly structured and closed *despite everything*.

In analyzing certain broad-ranging effects of this type of criticism, I saw that classical literary theory and the rhetorical approach consistently agreed on at least one point that impedes any consideration of the essay's specificity as an *a-generic* text or as *anti-genre*: they conceive of the determinable textual unities and singularities—that is, the particular quality of a text or of a literary genre—only as already empirically or formally imprisoned, realized in a supreme Self, a superior "I," or a closed Form. Where the essayist affirms practically that meaning must not set too quickly, that the text must not harden into *one* genre, criticism continued to seek out the Meaning, the End, the Beginning, the Origins.

By trying to define in detail the mode of the essay's functioning—and in particular by proposing the category of *Reflective Text*—my objective was twofold: on the one hand, it was a matter—thanks to this notion—of going beyond the canonical oppositions (discourse/story; narrative/discursive) without claiming to furnish a synthesis or to supersede the problematics of Genres: such as it is still today, it furnishes an excellent means of describing the classic text. On the other hand, it was also a matter, for me, of providing the means to account for the specificity of the essayistic text without having to resort to negative concepts: *in*completion, *in*exhaustivity, *il*limitability, *in*decidability, etc. The essay came to appear, then, as the appropriate instrument for a point of view that is impossible to represent, impossible to reduce to a schema, a table, or a determinate genre—or, as Blanchot would put it, the means of an essentially *plural* speech: that is, an intermittent, discontinuous speech which, "though not lacking signification, does not speak by reason of its power to represent, nor even to signify" but always *designates* itself "on the basis of the in-between [*entre-deux*]" as pure "space of dis-location that it tries to delimit, but which always discerns it, identifying it with this gap, an imperceptible interval, where it always comes back to it, identical, non-identical" (*L'Entretien infini*, 234–235).

I have taken a certain pleasure in representing and naming with the essayists themselves the impossible site of this gap: "sufficient word," "supernumerary emblem," or mana-word. I also assigned it an exoteric object: the multiple body of the "Society of Friends of the Text." A word, an object that began to proliferate vertically and horizontally *at the same time*: not like a finalized and hierarchized genealogical *tree*, but like an "abstract machine" capable of implementing the connection between a new language and the semantic and pragmatic ("practical") contents of the most heterogeneous utterances, of the collective arrangements of enunciation (Theater, Cinema, Radio, Television), and lastly a micropolitics of the social field (reading, writing):

> If I managed to talk politics *with my own body*, I should make out of the most banal of (discursive) structures a structuration; with repetition, I should produce Text. (*RB*, 175)

It is this *Text* that I wanted to explore and not merely describe under the category of "reflective text": I have sought to trace the map of this text so that I might move about freely in the *Essays* (of Montaigne, of Barthes) without any longer making the attempt to find *one* meaning, or a single model, or a unique direction. But this map can be read in an infinite number of ways: it can be torn up, turned upside down, reorganized; it can also be adapted to the most extraordinary montages, can be worked on by individuals, groups, or a social formation.

In this sense, one can say that the essay is not *a* genre like any other, and perhaps not a *genre* at all: first, because it is not *one*, but also because it no longer obeys the rule of the game: the rhetorical-juridical rule of genres. Indeed, for the essay it is no longer a question of recounting, nor of edifying, nor of instructing; it is a question now, perhaps, of provoking events (Deleuze and Guattari, *Rhizome*).

Nor is the essay a mixture of genres. It does not mix genres, it complicates them: the genres are, in a way, its "fallout," the historically determined actualizations of what is potentially woven into the essay. The latter appears, then, as the moment of writing *before* the genre, before genericness—or as the matrix of all generic possibilities.

What then is the essay? A question in the manner of Plato. What is the secret of its efficacy? What is its "genre?" Perhaps quite simply what Plato attributed to the art of the Sophist: "This art of contradiction which, by the ironical part of an art founded on mere opinion, belongs to mimicry and, by the genre that produces simulacra, is concerned with the making of images; this part, not divine but merely human, of the art of production, having discourse as its particular province, fabricates its illusions; such, it may be said, is the type and genre, the blood and lineage of the genuine sophist [Essayist]" (*The Sophist*, 268, c–d).

What if, instead of seeking the *essence* of the essay in vain, amid the hierarchy of existing modes and genres—and in particular between the discursive and the narrative—one posited the essay first, in order to let each of these modalities then be defined on the basis of it? What if, finally, like the Sophist, the Essay belongs in the last instance to the genre of the *Other* by which the *genres* communicate with each other? In this case, the difference between genres—like that between the sexes—will appear as secondary to us and the essayistic text as primary: then there would be no question of discursive and narrative except in relation to the text. It could no longer be said, as it has been said, that the essay is *neither* (completely) narrative, *nor* (completely) "logical." Nor, moreover, that it is *both narrative and discourse*—a "mélange" of genres.

In the logic of the Reflective Text, the essay would be neither non-being as Nothing nor being as Everything, but the figure of Alterity, the Other that generates all other (genres), the instigator of their Form, the cut that relates texts and languages and that makes this relation both necessary and impossible—"problematic"—since the essayist, like the Sophist, is always the one and the other, *écrivain* and *écrivant*, poet and theoretician: let us say a God, or rather a *Goddess*, as Barthes said: "a figure that can be invoked, a means of intercession" (*RB*, 64) or a progressive (processive) movement that constantly leads from language to poem and from poem to the body as a text—*corpus*—to decipher *as far as the eye can see*.

Appendix

Appendix
The Essay

Among all the terms that relate to literary genres, the word Essay is certainly the one that has given rise to the most confusion in the history of literature; since Montaigne used the term to describe his writings, "essay" has served to designate works that are so diverse from a formal point of view, and so heterogeneous from a thematic point of view, that it has become practically impossible to subsume a single, definitive type of text under this term. Since the 17th century, the lexeme *Essay* has been used to describe any prose text of medium length wherein an informal tone prevails and the author does not attempt an exhaustive treatment. This meaning goes back to the first edition of the *Dictionnaire de l'Academie* (1798): "This is still said of certain works called thus either by modesty or because the author did not propose to explore in depth the subject he treats." And, in fact, in contrast to the *Treatise* or *Summa*, *Essay* constantly refers to a wide variety of works that have nothing in common but the absence of system and a relative "brevity."

"Essays" are to be found in nearly all fields and all periods: in physics for example (*Essai sur la nature de l'air*, Mariotte, 1676), and also in botany (*Essais élémentaires sur la botanique*, J. J. Rousseau, 1771), in mineralogy (*Essai de mineralogie des Monts-Pyrenees*, Abbé Palasson, 1781), in mathematics (*Essai philosophique sur les probabilités*, Laplace, 1814) and quite obviously, in poetics (*L'air et les songes, Essai sur l'imagination du mouvement*, Gaston Bachelard, 1947) and in philosophy (*Essay on Human Understanding*, John Locke, among hundreds of others, 1690).

Today, the word Essay is still used to describe the most diverse and sometimes the most contradictory genres: under the Essay rubric are ranged autobiographical text, memoirs, journals, critical studies—exemplified by Sartre's *Situations* or Butor's *Repertoire(s)*—and even dialogues—for example, those of Plato or Diderot. Lukács's *Soul and Form* includes even Schopenhauer's *parerga* and practically all Kierkegaard's works within this category. Indeed, for a very long time, if a prose text represented a relatively personal point of view on any subject, it was automatically classified as an Essay.

Though infatuation for this term and its borrowing for the denomination of other genres is not unconnected with the considerable success and influence of Montaigne's *Essais* (1580–1588), it was not Montaigne who gave this term all the meanings it has carried since the Middle Ages. Coming from the Latin *exagium*, which signified both *exact weighing* and, by extension, *ordeal*, then *examination*, the lexeme *Essai* and the verb *Essaier* 'to try' already existed in commonly used locutions such as *faire l'essai* 'try out' or *mettre a l'essai* 'put to the test'. We know what Montaigne has made of this word and we can easily guess what philosophers, scholars, and writers will derive from it after the Renaissance: with the emergence of "experimental science" and philosophical taste for the concrete "observation" of "facts," a word like "essay" will become a most useful and precious term. A polysemic word par excellence, "essay" can designate at one and the same time a trial (experimental, moral, physical), an examination (of conscience or of resources) and an exercise, an athletic trial: thus, in the story of *Petit Jehan de Saintré*, we find: "to play ball, throw bars, rocks and fiery stakes, and all other essays" (Hamel 1959). The verb *essaier* 'to try', for its part, is also used in the language of corporations which demand that after six years of apprenticeship a worker must be *essaié* 'tried', that is, *judged* by the jury. *Essaier* is thus *mettre à l'essai* 'put to the test' and also, at the same time, *faire l'essai (l'experience) de, éprouver, et subir*: 'try out (experience), put to the test, and suffer' (Hamel, ibid.). Therefore, it is not surprising to see this term describe such heterogeneous "works," from the Renaissance to our own time: to write an Essay, it is enough to avoid a learned tone, to keep it "short," and to propose putting something (an idea, body, thing) to the test of one's own reflection.

As can be seen, use of the substantive "Essay" does not raise a major difficulty: insofar as it depends upon the decision—if not arbitrary, at least *contingent*—of a writer, it represents a historical event that one cannot help but ratify. On the other hand, the creation of the *genre* of Essay by Montaigne was not accomplished without problems. A unique case in the annals of literature, the Essay is the only literary genre to have resisted integration, until quite recently, in the taxonomy of genres. No other genre ever raised so many theoretical problems concerning the origin and the definition of its Form: an atopic genre or, more precisely, an *eccentric* one insofar as it seems to flirt with all the genres without ever letting itself be pinned down, the literary essay such as Montaigne bequeathed it to posterity has always had a special status. No doubt, by virtue of the multiplicity of contradictory principles governing its organization—the pace "by leaps and gambols" of its style, the absence of a unique or unified subject, its philosophical "incompleteness," its disrespect for the rhetorical norms of plan and progression, (in short, of composition)—Montaigne's *Essays* have not ceased to be the object of a mechanism of "disavowal" that historically has taken the following form: on the one hand, devalorization and rejection: "The essay is a degenerate, impossible genre, not very serious and even dangerous" (the attitude of Pascal and Malebranche, for example); and on the other hand, valorization and reappropriation: "Moreover, this belongs to me and I have always said so" (such is the attitude of Gide or Valéry). What is remarkable here is that in a systematic fashion the first argument generally bears on the "form" of the Essay and the second on its "content" (Boase 1935). This helps explain why the study of Montaigne's *Essays*—and through them, that of Genre—has always comprised two movements that have not always blended: a time in which the *philosophical* point of view prevailed (What is Montaigne's "thought"?) and one in which the *formal* and *generic* point of view dominated instead. As we know, if the first question received an incalculable number of "answers," the second was never directly taken into account until relatively recently. Indeed, if the much debated "thought" of Montaigne seems comparatively well "understood" today, the form of the genre and certain "supernumerary" and eccentric effects that it still enables the essay to produce at the expense of the most scrupulous commentator, continue to be the object of open debate.

In the books where the question of genre is tackled head on, the appearance of the Essay and its mode of organization are usually related to the general context from which the *Essays* emerged. The by now classic example of this type of approach is that of Pierre Villey (*Les sources et l'evolution des "Essais" de Montaigne*, 1908), who, analyzing the cultural and philosophical environment of the period when Montaigne composed his *Essays* makes them derivative of the multitude of genres and sub-genres that were still in fashion during the Renaissance: the *Adages* and *Apophtegmes* of Erasmus, the *Lectiones antigua* of Caellius Rhodiginus, the *Golden Letters* of Guevara, as well as the mass of compilations, commentaries, Lessons and *Moralia* that dominated the intellectual scene. In such a context, the *Essays* appear as the reaction, "in an overflowing century" (Montaigne), of the Renaissance man to the slightly dusty picture of classical Antiquity: it would be a matter of "making a new inventory," of taking new bearings and making a fresh start in thought. It is the existence of these "genres" that would explain, among other things, the variety of forms and the multiplicity of themes that traverse Montaigne's *Essays*: here, the Essay appears "incomplete" and "not composed" only to the "modern" mind. The Essay does not arise from a literary void, but from a "literary field" that has disappeared.

Much the same idea is found in Hugo Friedrich (1968), for whom the Essay appears as the manifestation of an "anti-scholastic" movement of liberation that explains and favors the emergence and the triumph of the "open form" and the "taste for mélanges."

Though such an approach can quite obviously account for a given thematic or stylistic aspect of the Essay, it nonetheless remains fundamentally extrinsic and far too descriptive. It is better at showing that which, in the Essay, belongs to other genres, than in concretely presenting what belongs to it alone.

In a more recent study, focusing on the history and the form of the Essay genre—which he assimilates to the more general notion of *self-portrait*—Michel Beaujour (1980) has tried to surmount these theoretical difficulties. He convincingly shows that, despite its incontestable utility, this type of interpretation nevertheless misses the essential: namely, the importance of the *rhetorical practice* in existence at the time the Essay first appeared. For Beaujour, that the Essay could be regarded for so long as a discourse without "origin" and "without precedent" is less because the contemporaneous sub-genres and the Essay's supposed transformation of them have been forgotten than because modern criticism has "repressed" the rhetorical "matrix" that conditioned the mode of functioning and the organization of *all* the genres of the Renaissance. It is this dimension that would explain, among other things, the *timeless* and *utopic* character of the Essay; standing out against the background of an absent structure stemming from the Commonplaces (*Loci*) of rhetorical *Inventio* and rhetorical Memory, it always reflects a "phantasm of community foreign to history" and a "subject" that is impersonal and transhistoric.

Hence the permanence of the Essay's *themes*—it is the Book of the Self confronting Value, the Imaginary, the Ideological, and the eternal return of Stupidity; hence the persistence of the Figures (*Figura*): Desire, Bliss, Death, the Body, Grief, Time, the Symbolic, etc. Thus, from Saint Augustine's *Confessions* to *Roland Barthes by Roland Barthes*, by way of Rousseau's *Reveries* or Nietzsche's *Ecce Homo*, if we do not always apprehend the *same* man, it is always the same "type of memory, both very archaic and very modern, by which the events of an individual life are eclipsed by the recollection of an entire culture" (Beaujour 1977). The "disorder" and the absence of philosophical completeness in the Essay are, in the final analysis, only apparent: distracted by Montaigne's anti-rhetorical attitude or by the modern (narcissistic) "prejudice" that makes us favor the *topoi* of "psychoanalytic vulgate" to the detriment of rhetorical *topoi*, we take for "poetic license" and radical originality what in reality is heavily coded. An adequate rhetoric is what we lack: the Essay is gibberish without origin only for those without Memory.

Less *empirical* in its proceedings, this approach permits us to render a better account of the most salient features of this "impossible" genre, the Essay, but it is not certain that it escapes the "reflex of reduction" (Sollers) that characterizes the other types of analyses. The Essay is, once more, related to a unique "origin," a unique "source." In other words, if it is true that when one negatively or privatively defines the Essay as an "incomplete" text, without order, etc., one only per-petuates the misunderstanding of the influence of rhetorical schemas; and if con-sequently it is necessary to return to these "sources," it nonetheless remains true that the Essay is not confined to pure and simple *repetition* of these schemas: a text that is not in appearance rhetorically "composed," the Essay is nonetheless a "constituted" text on the formal plane. Consequently, rather than merely taking an inventory of what it *owes* to Rhetoric, one must also show *at the same time* what it has done with this inheritance. Therefore, it is important to raise the capi-tal problem of the *general economy* of the essayistic text insofar as it constitutes a specific "work" and insofar as it has at its disposal an "operatory" power (Galay 1977) that is not homogeneous *with any preconceived rhetorical schema.*

Having renounced the economy of the philosophical "system" commanded by the idea of Mastery, and having dismissed the economy of Literary Genres inso-far as it commands the ordered exchange of the different modes of enunciation (narration or discourse), the Essay appears historically as one of the rare literary texts whose apparent principal task was to provoke a "generalized collapse" of the economies of the rhetorically coded text: in fact, what is most important to the essayist is neither the problem of *Invention*: finding something to say; nor that of rhetorical *Disposition*: putting in order what has been found (Barthes 1970); nor that of *Knowledge*: speaking Being, Truth, etc.; but, finally, that of *Compli-cation*. As Barthes says, in the spirit of Montaigne, it is a question "with intellec-tual things . . . of combining . . . *at the same time* theory, critical combat, and pleasure" (Barthes 1975). That is, outside the "presentative synthesis" that rhetoric offers and outside the philosophical system or Treatise ("closed," "mono-semic," and "dogmatic"), there remains, for the one who has renounced all Mas-tery, the possibility of a writing as "procedure," or as Barthes puts it a "tactics without strategy" (Barthes, ibid.). Together with the outlines, the written exer-cises, and the fussy precisions of composition, the entire "scene" of language as a warlike *Topos* and battlefield (of Faculties and Theses) is "gone beyond" in a deporting movement. Indeed, what offers food for thought, what allows us to ex-periment with the Essay as writing, as a unique Form, is the possibility of a "plu-ral" text made up of multiple networks "that interact without any one of them be-ing able to dominate the others": an "ideal" text that neither assumes an ultimate signified nor merely repeats the Same, but is a "galaxy of signifiers . . . it has no beginning; it is reversible; we gain access to it by several entrances, none of which can be authoritatively declared to be the main one" (Barthes 1970). In this sense, the Essay refers less to the genres and to the rhetorical repertoire—these are only two of the possible "entrances"—than to the power (*dunamis*) of the specific "procedures" that it brings into play in order to elaborate its rhetoric and to produce its effects (Galay, ibid.).

Born *practically* and *aesthetically* with Montaigne, and reappearing sporadi-cally in the history of literature (Beaujour 1980), the Essay still had to be born *theoretically*: with essayists like Nietzsche (for example *Ecce Homo*, the *Gay Science*), Paul Valéry (*Les Cahiers* or *Rhumbs* and *Tel Quel*) and above all recently with Roland Barthes, this genre judged "unclassifiable" for a long time, was finally able to make its "theoretical entrance" into the history of literature and the theory of literary genres.

Works Cited

Barthes, Roland. 1970. *S/Z*. Paris: Seuil, coll. "Tel Quel."

——. 1975. *Roland Barthes par Roland Barthes*. Paris: Seuil, coll. "Ecrivains de Toujours."

Beaujour, Michel. 1977. Autobiographie et autoportrait. *Poétique* 32, November.

——. 1981. *Miroirs d'encre, rhétorique de l'autoportrait*. Paris: Seuil.

Boase, Alan M. 1935. *The Fortunes of Montaigne: A History of the Essays in France, 1580–1669*. London: Methuen.

Friedrich, Hugo. 1975. *Montaigne*. Paris: Gallimard.

Galay, Jean Louis. 1977. Problèmes de l'oeuvre fragmentaire: Valéry. *Poétique* 31, September.

Hamel, S. 1959. "Expérience-Essai": Contribution à l'étude du vocabulaire de Montaigne. *Bibliothèque de la Société des Amis de Montaigne*, July–December: 20–32.

Abbreviations

In citing works in the foreword, the texts, and the notes, short titles have generally been used, including the following initials that refer to works by and about Roland Barthes. The French title and year of publication are given for books cited in their English translation. Unless otherwise indicated, translations of foreign-language quotations are my own – P. F.

CE   *Critical Essays*, trans. Richard Howard (Evanston, Illinois: Northwestern University Press, 1972). *Essais critiques*, 1964.

CL   *Camera Lucida: Reflections on Photography*, trans. Richard Howard (New York: Hill and Wang, 1981). *La Chambre claire*, 1980.

L   "Inaugural Lecture, Collège de France," trans. Richard Howard, in *A Barthes Reader*, ed. Susan Sontag (New York: Hill and Wang, 1982), 457–478. *Leçon inaugurale au Collège de France*, 1978.

LDF   *A Lover's Discourse: Fragments*, trans. Richard Howard (New York: Hill and Wang, 1978). *Fragments d'un discours amoureux*, 1977.

PRB   *Prétexte: Roland Barthes* [Colloque de Cerisy] (Paris: "10/18," 1978).

PT   *The Pleasure of the Text*, trans. Richard Miller (New York: Hill and Wang, 1975). *Le Plaisir du texte*, 1973.

RB   *Roland Barthes by Roland Barthes*, trans. Richard Howard (New York: Hill and Wang, 1977). *Roland Barthes par lui-même*, 1975.

SE   *Sollers écrivain* (Paris: Ed. du Seuil, 1979).

SFL   *Sade/Fourier/Loyola*, trans. Richard Miller (New York: Hill and Wang, 1976). *Sade/Fourier/Loyola*, 1971.

S/Z   *S/Z*, trans. Richard Miller (New York: Hill and Wang, 1974). *S/Z*, 1970.

TM   "The Third Meaning," in *Image-Music-Text*, ed. and trans. Stephen Heath (New York: Hill and Wang, 1977), 52–68. Included in *A Barthes Reader*. *"Le Troisième Sens,"* 1970. First published in *Cahiers du cinéma* 222, 1970.

Notes

Foreword

1. Roland Barthes, "Inaugural Lecture, Collège de France," trans. Richard Howard, in *A Barthes Reader*, 457–478. (Originally published in English in *October* 8 [Spring 1979], 3–15.)

2. See Phillip Lopate, "The Essay Lives – in Disguise," *New York Times Book Review* (November 18, 1984), 1; 47–49.

3. Roland Barthes, "Les Sorties du texte," in *Bataille* (Paris: U. D. G. "10/18," 1973), 48–62. Reprinted in Roland Barthes, *Le Bruissement de la langue: Essais critiques IV* (Paris: Ed. du Seuil, 1984). (Unless otherwise indicated, translations of foreign-language quotations are my own – M. R.)

4. Michel Leiris, "Alberto Giacometti," *Documents* 4 (Paris, 1929), 209–210.

5. Jean-Paul Sartre, "Un Nouveau Mystique," in *Situations I* (Paris: Gallimard, 1947), 143–188. (Originally published in *Cahiers du sud* [1943], 260–262.)

6. Roland Barthes, "La Métaphore de l'oeil. *Critique* 195–196 (1962), 772. Reprinted in *Critical Essays*, 239–247.

7. Francis Marmande, *Georges Bataille politique* (Doctorat d'Etat, Paris-VIII, 1982), 227.

8. Julia Kristeva's recent *"mémoire,"* cited in Note 9, is worth consulting for more information on this issue.

9. See *L'Infini* (Winter 1983), 39–54.

10. Pierre Klossowski, *Nietzsche et le cercle vicieux* (Paris: Mercure de France, 1969), 367.

11. In Barthes, *Le Bruissement*, 313–325.

12. Jacques Derrida, interview in *Le Nouvel Observateur* (Vendredi, 9 septembre 1983), 63.

13. Barthes, *Le Bruissement*, 325.

Introduction

1. Cited by Roland Barthes in The "Inaugural Lecture, Collège de France," in *A Barthes Reader*, 476.

2. I am thinking here of what Barthes wrote in *The Pleasure of the Text*: "No 'thesis' on the pleasure of the text is possible; barely an inspection (an introspection) that falls short. *Eppure si gaude!*" (34), and also of what he wrote regarding the "criticism" and "reading" of literary works in *Sollers écrivain*. See, in particular, the article entitled "Par-dessus l'épaule," 74ff.

3. "L'Envers des signes," *Figures I* (Paris: Ed. du Seuil, 1966), 185ff.

4. See "Authors and Writers," in *Critical Essays* (1972), reprinted in *A Barthes Reader*. Genette noted this movement of oscillation in Barthes when he wrote: "Therefore, literature for the semiologist (the critic) is a permanent temptation, a vocation that is ceaselessly postponed till later, and accomplished in this dilatory mode: like the Proustian narrator, the semiologist is a 'deferred author' " (*Figures I*, 204).

5. "Un Nouveau Mystique," *Situations I* (Paris: Gallimard, 1947), where the following can be read: "The contemporary novel, with the American authors, with Kafka, and in France with Camus, has found its style. *That of the essay remains to be found*. And I would also add: that of criticism . . ." (33).

6. On these questions, see Blanchot, *L'Entretien infini* (Paris: Gallimard, 1969) and the decisive work on the Romantics done by P. Lacoue-Labarthe and J. L. Nancy: *L'Absolu littéraire (Paris*: Ed. du Seuil, 1978).

7. I am thinking here of what Blanchot wrote concerning what we can call with Derrida the "Law of Genre": "Peculiarity of the Law: it is broken even though it is not uttered. . . . Whence it might be concluded that the law—such that, transmitted, supporting the transmission, it becomes the law of transmission—*constitutes itself as law only by the decision to break it*: there would be limit only if the limit is crossed, *revealed as uncrossable* by the crossing" (*L'Entretien*, 634). In addition, see Derrida's writing on the Blanchotian problematics of genre, in "The Law of Genre," *Glyph* 7 (Baltimore: Johns Hopkins Univ. Press, 1980).

8. See "International Colloquium on Genre," *Glyph* 7, Appendix, 234ff.

9. Ibid., 235.

10. Writing this, I separate myself from the analyses that F. Flahaut, for example, proposed for *S/Z* in the special issue of *Poétique* devoted to Barthes. See "Sur *S/Z* et l'analyse des récits," *Poétique* 47 (1981), 303ff. It seems to me, in fact, that, taking the "theses" of *S/Z* on the analysis of narratives at face value, Flahaut obviously has no difficulty in discerning a certain "vagueness" (312) in Barthes's use of a certain number of concepts that he "borrows" from the culture of the moment (psychoanalytic, structuralist, etc.): such notions as "symbol," "symbolic," "castration," etc. It is certainly the case that *taken literally and out of context*, all the concepts used by Barthes tend to depart from the rules of functioning that were theirs in the disciplines from which they were extracted. But as I shall try to show in this study—see, for example, Section 3, "Gestures of the Idea"—for Barthes a concept never has to be "honored" as such: therefore, it is through an altogether necessary movement that the most rigorous notions will be coefficiented by a margin of uncertainty, marked by a vagueness or fluidity totally foreign to the logic of theoretical discourse and classical assertive propositions. In rebaptizing concepts as "intellectual objects" from *S/Z* onward—see, in particular, *Roland Barthes*—Barthes shows that he is quite aware of the problems posed by an unorthodox use of theoretical concepts. I shall study this problem in greater detail later. For the time being, let me refer to Barthes's own clarification of the status of *S/Z* in his work and the "excessive" use of certain philosophical, psychoanalytic, etc., concepts. See, for example, the interview in *Le Grain de la voix* (Paris: Ed. du Seuil, 1981), 77-78: "My recourse to psychoanalytic language, as to any other idiolect, is ludic, citational—and I am convinced that this is so for everyone, with more or less good faith. We are never proprietors of a language. A language is only borrowed or "passed" like a disease or a coin. You saw how in *S/Z*, contrary to all deontology, I did not 'cite my sources' . . . this was to make it clear that, in my eyes the entire text, from beginning to end, is citational. I indicated this in my presentation by recalling the roles of *compilator* and *auctor* in the Middle Ages." See also page 80: "The vagueness of the concept does not have to be rectified by a consensus of competent readers; it is maintained by

the author's system, his idiolect, it is enough that the concepts fit together within the discourse, so that the other text, the tutor text, the object, whatever it may be, on the basis of which one writes, will be merely taken aslant by language and not scrutinized frontally." Concerning this major problem, see the fine article that Umberto Eco and Isabella Pezzini devoted to "La Sémiologie des *Mythologies*," in *Communications* 36, *numéro special sur R. Barthes* (Paris: Ed. du Seuil, 1982), 19–42.

11. My reasons for preferring "reflective" to other terms — to *reflexive*, for example — will become apparent in the pages that follow, but I would like to say this much here: "Reflexive" is not suitable because it accounts for only *one* of the aspects of what is at work in the genre of texts that Barthes began to produce after *S/Z*: namely, their "theoretical" side. Barthes was, moreover, completely conscious of the problem. In response to the question whether a "non-theoretical" work would not be "reactionary," he answered: "Julia Kristeva's work is viewed as theoretical; it *is* theoretical. However, it is viewed as theoretical in the sense of *abstract*, of *difficult*, because theory is believed to mean abstraction, difficulty. . . . But 'theoretical' does not mean 'abstract,' of course; from my point of view, it means *reflexive* — in other words, *that which returns upon itself*: a discourse that returns upon itself is by that very token theoretical. The eponymous hero, the mythical hero, of theoretical discourse could be Orpheus" (*Le Grain de la voix*, 136). As may be noted, if it lends itself essentially to *reflexivity* — to the return or turning upon itself of language — the term "reflexive" remains, despite everything, inextricably linked for Barthes to *theoretical* practice. Thus, the temptation to use it to describe what is at work in Barthes's later writings must be rejected.

"Reflective," however, aptly fulfills its function; on the one hand, because it *maintains a certain* ambiguity: in Barthesian terms, it is an *enantioseme*: it suggests "thought," reflexion, and *at the same time*, shimmering, reverberation, etc. On the other hand, it is rich in philosophical connotations. In his *Critique of Judgment*, Kant distinguishes two types of "judgment": (1) a judgment that directly concerns the *cognition* of objects; this type is what Kant calls a *determining* judgment. And (2) a judgment that consists essentially in a *reflexion* that the subject makes upon the functioning of his own mind and that refers only *indirectly* to the object, and this is what Kant calls a *reflective* judgment: "Judgment, in general," Kant writes in the *Critique of Judgment*," is the faculty of thinking the particular as contained under the universal. If the universal (the rule, the principle, the law) is given, then the judgment — which here subsumes the particular — is *determinant*. But if only the *particular* is given and the universal has to be found for it, then the judgment is *reflective*" (Introduction & IV). We see how such a register can be turned to account: Barthes's writing — I do not say "thought" — will preferably be called "reflective" in that, no longer selecting the "substantial objects" of knowledge (genres, literature, novel, etc.) and always basing itself on a *particular* object (a given text of Sade, given words of Fourier), it will deal only with "problematic" objects: Text, Bliss, Death. . . . Like *judgment* in the Kantian sense of the term, Barthes's writing has *reflective* principles as its principles, ones that apply essentially to our capacities to feel pleasure: "The text you write must prove to me *that it desires me*. This proof exists: it is writing. Writing is: the science of the various blisses of language, its Kama Sutra (this science has but one treatise: writing itself)" (*PT*, 6).

"Are there representations that determine *a priori* a subject's state as pleasure or pain?" A Kantian sort of question that Barthes took seriously, and which he believed he could answer by reviving essayistic writing. As one might guess, Barthes's "response" will owe nothing more to Kantianism. See Kant's *Critique of Judgment*, trans. J. C. Meredith (London: Oxford Univ. Press, 1980) and Deleuze's fine study, *Kant's Critical Philosophy*, trans. H. Tomlinson and B. Habberjam (Minneapolis: Univ. of Minn. Press, 1984).

12. See Leyla Perrone-Moises, "L'Intertextualite critique," in *Poétique* 27 (1976).

13. These have been masterfully demonstrated in books and studies to which I shall refer in due course. See, for example, M. Beaujour, "Autobiographie et autoportrait" in *Poétique* 32 (1977) and *Miroirs d'encre* (Paris: Ed. du Seuil, 1981). P. Lacoue-Labarthe and J. L. Nancy, *L'Absolu littéraire*, (Paris: Ed. du Seuil, 1978); A. Compagnon, *La Seconde Main*, (Paris: Ed. du Seuil, 1981).

14. Here I am thinking of what Barthes wrote in his preface to *Sade/Fourier/Loyola* and particu-

larly of this: "Were I a writer, and dead, how I would love it if my life, through the pains of some friendly and detached biographer, were to reduce itself to a few details, a few preferences, a few inflections, let us say: to 'biographemes' whose distinction and mobility might go beyond any fate and come to touch, like Epicurean atoms, some future body" (*SFL*, 9). Concerning the very particular status of the "detail" as "biographeme" that goes "beyond any fate," see Section 14 in this book, "Oh, a Friend!"

15. See, on these questions, J. L. Nancy, "Logodaedalus," in *Poétique* 21 (1975) and D. Kambouchner, "Le Labyrinthe de la Présentation," *Critique* 368 (1978).

16. See J. L. Galay, "Problèmes de l'oeuvre fragmentale: Valéry," *Poétique* 31 (1977), 347 and the texts of J. L. Nancy and P. Lacoue-Labarthe already cited.

The Barthes Effect

1. This "method" will be perfected in the course of writing the *Essays*, but it will never be abandoned for another. In fact, Montaigne posits the originality of his "art" right from the beginning of his work even if it is true that he affirms it broadly and systematically only with the major essays of the Third Book. See, for example, the essay "Of vanity" in Book III: "Because such frequent breaks into chapters as I used at the beginning seemed to me to disrupt and dissolve attention even before it was aroused . . . I have begun making them longer, requiring fixed purpose and assigned leisure" (Chapter 9, page 762).

References are to *The Complete Works of Montaigne: Essays, Travel Journals, Letters*, newly translated by Donald M. Frame (Stanford, California: Stanford Univ. Press, 1957). The translations in this text follow Frame's closely, with occasional more literal renderings when they are needed to make the line of thought in this book clear. References henceforth give book, chapter, and page, thus: III. 9, 762.

2. "A consideration upon Cicero," *Essays* I. 40, 185.

3. I am alluding here to the thesis by Elizabeth W. Wittkower—*Die Form der Essais von Montaigne* (Basel, 1955)—which attempts an analysis of the structure of Book III of Montaigne's *Essays* and according to which the book is essentially constituted by a regular alternation between, on the one hand, what Wittkower calls a "philosophische Betrachtung" (philosophical consideration) and on the other—in some respect illustrating the latter—a series of *exempla* (Beispiele) of different kinds: examples borrowed from the philosophical tradition (Beispieleüberlieferung); stories and anecdotes from historians and compilers (Beispiele historische); examples of *experience* taken from Universal Wisdom (Beispiele Erfahrung); and finally, examples coming from a typically Montaignian idiosyncrasy.

Such a study has the merit of approaching the analysis of the "contents" of the *Essays* in constant relation with that of its form of organization and functioning, but at the price of a certain blindness: (1) it evades the problem of overdetermination of any "philosophical consideration" by the series of *exempla* of all sorts accompanying it; (2) it does not take into account the specific effect of the *distribution* of these examples in series that are not homogeneous; (3) it does not establish any qualitative distinction or formal hierarchy among the latter.

It is as if the text did no more than passively illustrate monological "theses"—Ideas—by a series of facts, stories, and examples that are relatively neutral. Regarding this aspect, see the essential critique by R. Etiemble of Wittkower's thesis in "Sens et structure dans un essai de Montaigne," *C.A.I.E.F.* 14 (1962).

4. See P. Lacoue-Labarthe and J. L. Nancy, *L'Absolu littéraire*, pages 58, 62, 200, 269, 384. See especially page 62: "The fragment is also a literary term: already in the eighteenth century, even in Germany, 'fragments' were published that resembled closely enough, so far as their form was concerned, essays in the Montaignian manner. 'Fragment' designates an exposition that makes no claim to exhaustiveness, and it corresponds to the doubtlessly quite modern idea that the unfinished work

can or even should be published (or to the idea that what is published is never altogether finished)."
I shall return later to the problem of the constant recourse to notions of incompleteness and inexhaustibility in order to define the essay as specific genre or text.

5. M. Baraz, "Les Images dans les *Essais*," in *B.H.R.* 27 (1965), 361–394.

6. See V. Goldschmidt, *Les Dialogues Platoniciens*, (Paris: P.U.F., 1960).

7. Therefore, it is neither a "philosophical consideration" nor the principle of "association of ideas" that can give an "order"—a single one—to the essayistic text. The first is only a "fallout," the second only a surface effect of the implementation of the "system" that governs the organization of the heterogeneous elements in the essay.

8. See Barthes, *Communications* 16 (1970) Sections B.O. 5, B.1.18 and J. L. Galay, "Problèmes de l'oeuvre fragmentale: Valéry," *Poétique* 31 (1977), 354, where it is clearly shown that what Valéry, contrary to Montaigne, "asks of rhetoric is not that, once a subject is imposed on him, rhetoric furnish him with reflections, but that it help him to present what is already at his disposal." But perhaps this is no longer the case for the Valéry of the *Cahiers*, who is much closer to the "impulsive" Montaigne of the *Essays*.

9. R. Jasinski, "Sur la composition chez Montaigne," in *Mélanges d'Histoire Litteraire offerts à Henri Chamard* (Paris, 1951).

10. When, at the beginning of the seventeenth century, attention was paid to the *Essays*, it was already in an "apologetic" form. Montaigne's disciples—but is Montaigne the kind of author who has disciples?—are forced to travesty the master's "thought" and "manner" in order to explain him: Pierre Charoon, for example, in his *Sagesse* gives a new rehash of the *Essays*: he makes the text into a *thought*, and to make it accepted in those orderly times, he systematizes it: the scattered fragments are regrouped by themes; digressions—or what are considered as such—are eliminated, contradictions are erased. Better yet: when the *Essays* are re-edited in 1677, it is with a new title—"Esprit des Essais," namely, a sort of *Digest*—and, above all, in a new form (an expurgated form). As P. Villey points out in his book on Montaigne: "digressions" are trimmed according to completely arbitrary criteria; titles are modified in order to "adapt" them to the content; long passages of the text are even cut out in order to make the content fit the title; finally, "L'Apologie de Raymond de Sebonde" is reduced to a few watered-down pages.

It should also be recalled that whereas between 1600 and 1669 there were no fewer than thirty-five editions of the *Essays*, from 1669 to 1724—during the period of the formation of "Classicism" as A. Thibaudet notes in his *Physiologie de la critique*—no new edition of the *Essays* was published. As Villey comments—without, however, deriving any lesson for determining the genre: "The growing taste for regularity banished the *Essays*." The *Essays*, just as they are, thus constitute a good example of an unclassifiable text. When it is not censored, Montaigne's work is transformed in order to give it an acceptable "appearance."

11. As A. Compagnon—*La Seconde Main* (Paris: Ed. du Seuil, 1981)—has well shown, this is obviously the mark of a "characteristic refusal of the universal of essence and even of genre," but also, above all, a categoric affirmation of the *ontologically primary* character of multiplicity and of Chaos. Elsewhere, Compagnon aptly remarks: "In such a universe of *essential diversity*, of radical contingency, as soon as no reality is recognized by entities other than *accidents*, what sort of discourse is still possible?" ("L'Imposture," in *Prétexte: Roland Barthes*, 48ff.) Proceeding from different premises, I am trying to answer the same type of questions in this section of the book.

12. Numerous studies have shown what status the *Essays* give to reader and author respectively. See in particular the fine article by M. Charles on pages 297–298 of his *Rhétorique de la lecture* (Paris: Ed. du Seuil, 1977) entitled, "Sur une phrase de Montaigne."

13. G. Deleuze, *Différence et répétition* (Paris: P.U.F., 1969), Répétition pour elle-même," 153ff.

14. See ibid., and *Logique du sens* (Paris: Ed. de Minuit, 1969), particularly series 6, 7, 8.

15. Deleuze, *Logique du sens*, 63ff.

16. In Nietzsche, there are many proper names that act as mana-words: Dionysus, Apollo, Ariadne, and of course Zarathustra. But what is remarkable is that whenever Nietzsche wants to designate the source of the "instinct"—or "taste," as he puts it—that secretly guided and inspired his work, he himself always has recourse to the same word: the word "body": *"Guided by the conducting thread of the body*, as I said, we learn that our life is only possible thanks to the play of numerous intelligences of very unequal value, therefore, to a perpetual exchange between obedience and command in countless forms" (*The Will to Power*; this fragment is admirably commented upon by B. Pautrat, in *Versions du soleil* [Paris: Ed. du Seuil, 1971], 269).

In Barthes, as in Nietzsche, it is never the *conscience* ("proud and chimerical," as Nietzsche says in *Ecce Homo*) that rules, but an unconscious, "enigmatic" force—or forces. (In *RB*, Barthes speaks of a "corporal enigma.")

17. Here, I depart appreciably from Beaujour's theses on the "self-portrait essay" in "Autobiographie et autoportrait" (*Poétique* 32 [1977]). I do not believe that the essay is "first a *found object* on which the writer confers the self-portraiture intention in the process of development," or that the essayist never clearly knows "where he is going or what he is doing" (*Poétique* 32, 444). I feel, on the contrary, that one must consider the self-portrait essay as an "object" manufactured like a machine or woven like a "plot," thereby demanding of the essayist a very substantial literary awareness of what he is doing! Far from enjoying great lucidity concerning his "ontological and moral stake" together with a profound ignorance of the rhetorical machine at work, the essayist relies on the machine and puts it to use. For more on this topic, see Stephen Heath's excellent book, *Vertige du déplacement* (Paris: Fayard, 1974), in particular the chapter entitled "Le Déplacement," 17–25.

18. As examples, Barthes gives us the drawing of Mount Fuji or the sardine that has just broken the line of words written in Japanese haiku. And see *RB*, 187, "The Signifier without the Signified" and "Doodling," and 128, "The History of Semiology."

19. There are a number of them in Barthes's discourse: the German *Abgrund* and *Aufhebung*, the English *Fading*, etc.

20. *Roland Barthes* and *A Lover's Discourse* aptly illustrate this: all the possible genres compete—letter, address, novel, philosophical reflection, etc.

21. For a semiology of "heterotopia," see G. Genot, "L'Adieu d'Ophélie," *Revue d'Esthetique* 3-4 (Paris: "10/18," 1978).

22. See M. Tort, "L'Effet-Sade," *Tel Quel* 28 (Winter 1967).

23. Barthes, "Writers, Intellectuals, Teachers," in *Image-Music-Text* (New York: Hill and Wang, 1977), 190–215 and *A Barthes Reader*, 378-403.

24. On the notion of Neutral in general, see *RB*, 132–133 and L. Marin's theoretical clarification in *Utopiques: Jeux d'espaces*, "Du Neutre pluriel et de l'utopie" (Paris: Ed. de Minuit, 1973). See also D. Wilhelm's *Maurice Blanchot: la voix narrative* (Paris: "10/18," 1974).

25. In here comparing the mode of constitution of the essayistic text with that of the philosophical system, I am thinking of the hypothesis proposed by Hugo Friedrich in his *Montaigne* (Paris: Gallimard, 1975) according to which one of the best possible approaches to a definition of the "logic" at work in the (Montaignian) essay is based on the definition of the philosophical "system." In fact, from the first chapter of his analysis of the Essays, Friedrich tries to show that when one takes one's point of departure from the definition that Kant, for example, gives of *system* in philosophy, a certain number of elements that critics had more or less brought to the fore, but in a disorganized manner, can be inferred. On the basis of a given definition—"I understand by system the unity of cognitions realized *under an idea*; the latter is the rational concept of the form of a whole, inasmuch as this concept determines *a priori* both the multiple expanse and the interrelation of its parts. . . . The whole is *articulated* and not accumulated (*Coacervatio*), it can increase internally but not externally"—it is easy for Friedrich to make a number of the major features of the essay appear. They appear "negatively," it is true, but much more convincingly than with many other critics. Through this detour, Friedrich shows that it is obvious that in any essay, *no* prior unity of knowledge or faculties is

demanded. According to him, the essay is characterized, on the contrary, by the liberty it maintains in the "vagueness of suppositions," as he puts it, as well as in the "multiplicity of points of view" and of ideas that it implements without ever risking a totalization. There seems to be no given unity or preestablished totality in an essay. Another reversal appears pertinent here: the specificity of the essayistic mode of exposition–of the *Darstellung*. Whereas the system proceeds *per articulatio*– through the regular linking of knowledge and in the perspective of the closure of a rational knowledge–the mode of presentation and exposition of the essay proceeds rather *per accumulatio* and consequently can increase "externally," by aggregation. On these questions, see J. L. Nancy, "Logodaedalus," in *Poétique* 21 (1975), and D. Kambouchner, "Le Labyrinthe de la présentation," *Critique*, 368 (Paris: Ed. de Minuit, 1978).

26. M. Tort, "L'Effet-Sade."

27. I am thinking of Nietzsche's fine text: "In the evolution of the spirit it is a question perhaps of nothing other than the body: it is *history* becoming aware that it forms a *superior body*. . . . Our yearning for knowledge of nature is a means through which the body tries to perfect itself–or rather: hundreds of thousands carry out experiments in order to modify the diet, the manner of dress, the way of life of the body: in it, consciousness and appreciation of values, all kinds of pleasure and displeasure are the *indices of these modifications*. . . . In the final analysis, it is not at all a question of man: he must be overcome." (Nietzsche, *Posthumous Fragments*, cited by P. Klossowski, *Nietzsche et le cercle vicieux* [Paris: Mercure de France, 1969], 59).

28. Such as Barthes defines it in *SFL*, 93: "Namely, the superimpression (in dual hearing) of two languages that are ordinarily foreclosed to each other, the braid formed by two classes of words whose traditional hierarchy is not annulled, balanced, but–what is more subversive–disoriented . . . , a sudden contagion *deranges* the institution of language."

29. On the notion of *emblem*, see Falhaut's article in *PRB*, "La Limite entre la vie et la mort," 76.

30. A. Robbe-Grillet, "Pourquoi j'aime Barthes," in *PRB*.

31. See, again, the text of Nietzsche's cited in Note 27 above.

32. There is a striking analogy with Blanchot's remarks concerning Nietzsche's fragmentary style: ("Juxtaposed words, but whose arrangement is entrusted to signs that are modes of space and that make space a play of relations where time is at play: they are called signs of punctuation. . . .) On the one hand, their role is one of impetus; on the other (and this is the same), of suspense, etc." (*L'Entretien infini*, 25).

33. See J. L. Galay, "Problèmes" (*Poétique* 31), 350.

34. See M. Beaujour, "Autobiographie et autoportrait" (*Poétique* 32), and Frances A. Yates, *The Art of Memory* (Chicago: Univ. of Chicago Press, 1974).

35. Barthes would have certainly taken up Goethe's protest to Eckermann: "Composition, what a vile word! We owe it to the French and we must rid ourselves of it as soon as possible. How can it be said that Mozart 'composed' *Don Juan*? Composition!" Quoted by Blanchot, *L'Entretien infini*, 473.

36. See *SFL*, 109–110 and *PT*–for example, 31.

37. J. L. Galay, "Problèmes," 351, note 17.

38. Malcolm Lowry, *Au-dessous du volcan*, trans. Stephen Spriel in collaboration with C. Francillon and M. Lowry (Paris: Editions Corrèa, 1950). See also G. Deleuze, *Logique du sens*, 182ff.

39. G. Deleuze, *Logique du sens*, 51; the entire content of this paragraph is dependent on Deleuze's very fine analysis of the notion of "intensive system."

40. "Any classification you read," writes Barthes, "provokes a desire in you to put yourself into it somewhere: where is your place? At first you think you have found it, but gradually, like a *disintegrating* statue or an *eroding* relief, its shape blurs and fades, or better still, like Harpo Marx losing his artificial beard in the glass of water he is drinking out of, you are no longer classifiable, not out of an excess of personality, but on the contrary because you pass through all the fringes of the phantom" (*RB* 143–144, emphasis mine).

41. See, for example, Blanchot's elaborations of the *Neutral* in the chapter entitled "Le Neutre, le fragmentaire": "*Neutral*: this extra word which is taken away, whether by reserving itself a place in which it is always soon lacking by marking itself there, whether by provoking a displacement without place, whether by distributing itself in a multiple manner in a supplement of place" (*L'Entretien infini*, 45).

42. See *RB*, 90-91, "The Double Figure": "This work, in its discontinuity, proceeds by means of two movements: the *straight line* (advance, increase, insistence of an idea, a position, a preference, an image) and the *zigzag* (reversal, contradiction, reactive energy, denial, contrariety, the movement of a Z, the letter of deviance)." See also page 89: "On the spiral's trajectory, everything recurs, but in another, higher place: it is then the return of difference, the movement of metaphor; it is Fiction." See also pages 70, 126, 158.

It is impossible here not to think of the analogies between essayist and composer. In particular, the relation between the musical text – also atopic and furthermore non-signifying (*asignifiant*) or insignifying (*insignifiant*) – and the procedures of the essayistic composition: reversal, transposition, repetition, imitation. Like the mana-word, the theme is "not yet a bit of melody, but a *tonal state* involving all sorts of melodic, rhythmic, and harmonic elements. The original cell has been molded like clay, retouched, drawn out, modeled. And to set against this first donnée, one has had to seek out other figures which resemble it and which do not resemble it, which are properly associated with it and which furnish at the same time new resources for development." (J. Samson, *Musique et vie intérieure*, 99-100, quoted by J. Berthélémy, *Traité d'esthétique* [Paris: Ed. de l'Ecole, 1964], 247.)

43. See G. Deleuze, *Différence et répétition*, 153ff.

44. Ibid., 159.

45. See "Linguistic allegories," *RB*, 123-124: "*This is a constant procedure in your work*: you use a pseudo-linguistics, a metaphorical linguistics: not that grammatical concepts seek out images in order to express themselves, but just the contrary, because these concepts *come to constitute allegories, a second language, whose abstraction is diverted to fictive ends*." (Emphasis mine.)

46. When he tries to characterize the "logic" at work in the fascination and particular interest that certain photographs evoke in him – namely the logic connecting the *studium* of a photo to its *punctum* – this word ("break") returns spontaneously to Barthes: "The second element [*punctum*] will break (or punctuate) the studium. This time it is not I who seek it out . . . , it is this element which rises from the scene, shoots out of it like an arrow, and pierces me" (*Camera Lucida*, 49). I shall return to the nature of such a "logic" as to the power of the *punctum* to fascinate; for the moment, I shall simply note the *insistent, systematic* character of the rule at stake: like the "modern" text, the photo can be evaluated – have a certain value – only insofar as it mobilizes two heterogeneous worlds, two discontinuous elements that communicate through a *ponctuel* ("pin-point," "punctual") atopic element that is nonetheless indiscernible. Derrida gives a very fine analysis of the play between *studium* and *punctum* in "Les Morts de Barthes," in *Poétique* 47 (1981), 269-292.

47. See J. L. Galay, "Problèmes," 361. And in particular: "The assimilation of the fragment to the idea of *germ* must be criticized, inasmuch as the latter implies the notion of an organic growth."

48. It is perhaps not superfluous to recall here the manner in which Barthes reads certain texts. In a text on Bataille, he writes: "Bataille presents two knowledges: an endoxal knowledge, that of Salomon Reinach and the editorial committee of *Documents* . . . and a more distant knowledge produced by Bataille (by his personal culture)." But Barthes is quick to add: "In this discourse of the second knowledge the reference is twofold: that of the foreign (of the elsewhere) and that of the detail; thus begins the disturbance of knowledge (of its law) by its futilization, its miniaturization!" ("Les Sorties du texte," in *Bataille* [Paris: "10/18," 1973], 51).

49. The following passage from *Camera Lucida* is, for me, a confirmation of the connections I make here between the notions of detail, linguistic allegory, obtuse meaning, *punctum* and haiku in Barthes: "A detail overwhelms the entirety of my reading; it is an intense mutation of my interest, a fulguration. By the mark of *something*, the photograph is no longer anything whatever. This *some-*

thing has triggered me, has provoked a tiny shock, a *satori*, the passage of a void (it is of no importance that its referent is insignificant). A strange thing: the virtuous gesture which seizes upon 'docile' photographs (those invested by a simple *studium*) is an idle gesture . . . ; on the contrary, the reading of the *punctum* (of the pricked photograph, so to speak) is at once brief and active. A trick of vocabulary: we say 'to develop a photograph'; but what the chemical action develops is undevelopable, an essence (of a wound), what cannot be transformed but only repeated under the instances of insistence (of the insistent gaze). This brings the Photograph (certain photographs) close to the haiku. For the notation of a haiku, too, is undevelopable: everything is given, without provoking the desire for or even the possibility of a rhetorical expansion. In both cases we might (we must) speak of an *intense immobility*: linked to a detail (to a detonator), an explosion makes a little star on the pane of the text or of the photograph: neither the Haiku nor the Photograph makes us 'dream' " (*CL*, 49).

50. This aspect of the matter shows the close relationship between poetic writing and "essayistic" writing. In fact, of the "essay," that is, of the reflective text such as Barthes re-invents it after Montaigne, one could say word for word what Blanchot says of the status of the image in the poem: "In the poem everything is image and everything makes itself image. And at the same time it must be said that every image is also the whole poem—its only center, its absolute and momentary apparition, its particular preference, its reservoir" (*L'Entretien infini*). See also J. L. Galay, "Problèmes," 361–362, where the links between the "fragmental text" and the "poetic text" are meticulously traced.

51. All these examples are taken from A. Lavers's article, "En traduisant Barthes," *Tel Quel* 47 (Autumn 1971).

52. Note what Barthes says about locating or deciphering the *punctum*: "In order to perceive the *punctum*, no analysis would be of any use to me (but perhaps memory sometimes would, as we shall see): it suffices that the image be large enough, *that I do not have to study it* (this would be of no help at all), that, given right there on the page, I should receive it right here in my eyes" (*CL*, 42–43, emphasis mine).

53. Of interest is Barthes's analysis in *Camera Lucida* of the way a photo of Wessing's is constituted and functions, and in particular this: "The scene [*tableau*] is in no way 'composed' according to a creative logic; the photograph is doubtless dual, but this duality is the motor of no 'development,' as happens in classical discourse" (*CL*, 42).

54. See Blanchot, *L'Entretien infini*, 440: "The neutral is what is not distributed in a genre: the non-general, the non-generic as the non-particular."

55. For an interesting view of how Bataille relates to the problem stemming from the necessity of writing a dictionary occupied with the "work" of words, see D. Hollier, *La Prise de la Concorde* (Paris: Gallimard, 1974), 63–64: "To privilege the sense at the expense of work is to believe that this practice [work] can be put in parentheses. Work (the word itself sounds contemptible) is not usage. . . . The word is then the site of an event, explosion of an affective potential, and not a means of expression of the sense. To write is to arrange around it the *void* which permits its charge of energy to rupture and shake the accumulation of sense."

56. See Blanchot, *L'Entretien infini*, 453ff.

57. See G. Genette, *Figures III* (Paris: Ed. du Seuil, 1972), 105–114.

58. M. Charles, *Rhétorique de la lecture*, 85.

59. I am alluding to Galay's final remark in "Problèmes de l'oeuvre fragmentale: Valéry" concerning Paul Valéry: "The author who turns such a product (the *Cahiers*) over to the public shows the confidence he has in himself, in the *identity of his spirit*, the confidence he must assume in his public." Here the category of genius will serve as return to a productive origin. But the problem remains the same: the unity and unicity of the author refer to a confidence which one has in oneself, which the public must share.

60. This is well demonstrated by Beaujour. See "Autobiographie et autoportrait" (*Poétique* 32), 447.

61. In this sense, what Genette says of the Baroque writer might be said of the essayist: he "lives

his rhetoric," and his work is only the unfolding of the latter. (*Figures I* [Paris: Ed. du Seuil, 1966], 214ff.)

62. See *SFL*, 8: "For if, through a twisted dialectic, the Text, destroyer of all subject, contains a subject to love, that subject is dispersed, somewhat like the ashes we strew into the wind."

63. "The reading must also be plural, that is, without order of entrance: the 'first' version of a reading must be able to be its last, as though the text were reconstituted in order to achieve its artifice of continuity, the signifier then being provided with an additional feature: shifting" (*S/Z*, 15).

64. In this sense, the essay as reflective text constitutes one of the forms that comes closest to the romantic ideal of the work: "romantic art" or "total novel," which most romantics were content to dream of in the form of *Märchen* or fragments of the Athenaeum but which the essayist could realize.

65. "With intellectual things, we produce simultaneously theory, critical combat, and pleasure; we subject the objects of knowledge and discussion—as in any art—no longer to an instance of truth, but to a consideration of effects" (*RB*, 90).

66. See M. Tort, "L'Effet-Sade," 75.

67. "Can one—or at least could one ever—begin to write without taking oneself for another? For the history of sources we should substitute the history of figures: the origin of the work is not the first influence, it is the first posture: one copies a role, then, by metonymy, an art: I begin producing by reproducing the person I want to be" (*RB*, 99).

68. See, in *RB*, the fragment entitled "The Privileged Relationship" (65): "He did not seek out an exclusive relationship (possession, jealousy, scenes); nor did he seek out a generalized, communal relationship; what he wanted was, each time, a privileged relationship, marked by a perceptible difference, brought to the condition of a kind of absolutely singular affective inflection, like that of a voice with an incomparable timbre."

69. See Barthes, "L'Image," in *PRB*, 298-309.

70. See, in *RB*, the fragments entitled "The Thrill of Meaning" (97-98) and "Phases" (145). See also Julia Kristeva's article in *Communications* 37 (1982), a special number devoted to Barthes: "La Voix de Barthes," 119-125.

Without attempting here to analyze the "politics" of the sign in Barthes, I will content myself with pointing out only that which is directly related to the strategy of writing generally adopted by Barthes after *The Pleasure of the Text*.

71. See *RB*, 65: "What was wanted was a plural equality, without in-difference."

72. Nietzsche, *Ecce Homo*, trans. Walter Kaufmann, in *On The Genealogy of Morals* and *Ecce Homo*, ed. Kaufmann (New York: Vintage Books, 1967).

73. See *PT*, 42-43: "The stereotype is the word repeated without any magic, any enthusiasm, as though it were natural, as though by some miracle this recurring word were adequate on each occasion for different reasons, as though to imitate could no longer be sensed as an imitation: an unconstrained word that claims consistency and is unaware of its own insistence. Nietzsche has observed that 'truth' is only the solidification of old metaphors. So in this regard the stereotype is the present path of 'truth,' the palpable feature which shifts the invented ornament to the canonical, constraining form of the signified." Note (in *The Pleasure of the Text*) the systematic way in which Nietzsche is invoked *whenever* the nature of any representation that passes through language is under investigation.

74. See *PT*, pages 13, 28, 33, 40, 42, 57, 61, 62. On all these pages, Barthes refers directly to Nietzsche whom he quotes, mentions, or "translates" freely. A detailed study in the incorporation of the Nietzschean problematics of values, sign, and subject in the work of the "later" Barthes is needed. I will merely situate the parameters that best permit rendering an account of the Barthesian "essays."

75. See Klossowski, *Nietzsche*, 115-137.

76. Barthes, "L'Image," in *PRB*—for example, 301-302.

77. I am thinking in particular of this passage from the Inaugural Lecture: "There is an age at which we teach what we know. Then comes another age at which we teach what we do not know;

this is called *research*. Now perhaps comes the age of another experience; that of *unlearning*, of yielding to the unforeseeable change which forgetting imposes on the sedimentation of the knowledges, cultures, and beliefs we have traversed. This experience has, I believe, an illustrious and outmoded name, which I now simply venture to appropriate at the very crossroads of its etymology: *Sapientia*: no power, a little knowledge, a little wisdom, and as much flavor as possible" (*L*, 478).

78. This is a constant theme in Barthes, but never better "treated" than in *Camera Lucida*. I am thinking in particular of this quite sublime passage: "In Brecht, by a reversal I used to admire a great deal, it is the son who (politically) educates the mother; yet I never educated my mother, never converted her to anything at all; in a sense, I never 'spoke' to her, never 'discoursed' in her presence, for her; we supposed, without saying anything of the kind to each other, that the frivolous insignificance of language, the suspension of images must be the very space of love, its music" (*CL*, 72).

Index

Index

Theory and History of Literature

Réda Bensmaïa is associate professor of French and comparative literature at the University of Minnesota. Currently, he is director of the Interuniversity Center for Film and Critical Studies in Paris. Bensmaïa has contributed to such journals as *Enclitic*, *Sub-Stance* and *Poétique*.

Pat Fedkiew is a graduate student in French at the University of Minnesota.

Michèle Richman is associate professor of French at the University of Pennsylvania and author of *Reading Georges Bataille: Beyond the Gift*.